Global Digital Economy and the 11th Plan ICT Equity Issues

Global Digital Economy and the 11th Plan ICT Equity Issues

P C Bodh

AUTHORSPRESS

Worldwide Circulation through Authorspress Global Network
First Published 2009
by
Authorspress
E-35/103, Jawahar Park
Laxmi Nagar, Delhi-110 092
e-mail: authorspress@yahoo.com

Global Digital Economy and the 11th Plan ICT Equity Issues
ISBN 978-81-7273-519-7

Printed in India at Tarun Offset, Delhi.

Acknowledgement

My hearty gratitude is due to a long list of people. Right from the occurrence of the idea about doing a research study on the digital economy to marking the course of action to translate it into a research work; and, finally, to writing a book on the basis of this research work, at every stage, colleagues and friends have contributed generously. Foremost among these is Dr. C. Murali Krishan Kumar, Adviser, Communication and Information Division, Planning Commission, New Delhi, who suggested to work on the digital technological convergence issues. I am also indebted to Prof. Sushma Yadav of IIPA for the guidance she rendered me in understanding the socio-economic inequality issues.

I am also grateful to Professor Rakesh Gupta of Indian Institute of Public Administration (IIPA) for his guidance in completing the basic research work as a part of my course in the Advance Professional Programme in Public Administration (APPPA) 2007-08 at Indian Institute of Public Administration.

I must express my deep gratitude to Shri B.S. Baswan, the Director, IIPA, who had been an inspiration to me; and Shri V.K. Sharma, the Course Director of the APPPA programme.

Finally, I must acknowledge my sincere gratitude to Shri Ram Krishan, Shri Amit Kumar and Shri Jaswant Singh for their enthusiastic involvement in conducting the pre-survey discussions with the sample population, and canvassing the questionnaires.

P C Bodh

Preface

The entry of India in the digital world economy with its rapidly growing information communication technology has raised issues beyond the global context and concern. Not only understanding the global digital divide between the advanced countries and the less developed, but also probing how the digital technology-enabled development affects the inequality-stricken socio-economic fabric of India should be the concern of Indian economy? Will the flow of digital information communication technology gains further sharpen the disparities? Will the educationally, economically, socially, and spatially-deprived, disadvantaged, lots of the deserts, of the forests, and of the mountains, be worse off, suffering wider gaps between them and the rest.

The book, first, takes up this issue by systematically studying the nature and structure of the world digital economy. The effort here is to understand the trend, the challenges, and the socio-economic problems and their solutions, so that lessons can be drawn for building the path ahead in the Indian scenario. In this section, the major technological, economic and social themes are discussed; the issues of digitalisation, shift to complete digital scenario, and the emerging trends of internetworked economy, internetworked news and media, governance and learning, and new economic issues, are examined.

Once the complexity of the digital world economy order is understood, the Indian scene of digital development plans is scanned. The Indian digital development agenda is examined for understanding the government's strategy to develop the country into a digital economy with full manifestation of the benefits of ICT in the development of the country's economy. In this, the IT and the telecommunication and the mass communication, everything under the plan was examined. The focus, however, was on probing into their likely effect on the socio-economic issues of the less developed lots. Not only the 11th Plan ICT content, but also their social and economic issues were analysed in a different section of the book for better planning lessons. Key issues concerning e-Governance, Research and Development in IT, e-health, e-agriculture and the priority on digitalisation of the content are discussed.

Preparedness of the socio-economically disadvantaged for entry into the glittering global digital world alone will determine how effectively India will be able to cash in on the digital world economy opportunities. It was for this that a case study of Delhi was carried out, and its results analysed. The data obtained from the study was used in developing a ten-point digital/IT conduciveness scale for finding the relative picture of the urban, semi-urban; and rural segments of Delhi.

The case study was carried out with the objective to ascertain how the economic, literacy, and spatial status of a social segment affect its ability to adapt to the digital socio-economic milieu; and to find out solutions to the problems; and to suggest policy prescriptions to resolve the 11th Plan inclusiveness issues.

P C Bodh

List of Acronyms

ADSL	Asymmetrical Digital Subscriber Loop
AIR	All India Radio
BPO	Business Processing Organisation
BPL	Broadband on Power Line
BSNL	Bharat Sanchar Nigam Limited
C&S	Cable and Satellite
CDB	Code Data Base
CUG	Closed User Group Communication
CSC's	Common Service Centres
CS	Counter Strike
DOS	Data Operating System
DARC	Data Radio Channel
DTH	Direct to Home
DOT	Department of Telecommunication
FAB	Mega Fabrication Unit
FDI	Foreign Direct Investment
GER	General Enrolment Rate
GRE	Graduate Rating Examination
GCH	General Category High Income
GCM	General Category Medium Income
GCL	General Category Low Income
HMCP	Hardware Manufacturing Cluster Parks
HDTV	High Definition Television

HITS	Head-end in the Sky
HMIS	Hospital Management Information System
HRD	Human Resource development
IT	Information Technology
ICT	Information Communication Technology
ITES	Information Technology Enabled Services
ICDS	Integrated Child Development Scheme
IPTV	Internet Protocol Television
ICE	Information, Communication, and Entertainment
ISRO	Indian Space Research Organization
IBP	Internet Backbone Provider
ISP	Internet Service Provider
IPR	Intellectual Property Rights
JSS	Jan Swasthya Sahyog
KPO	Knowledge Processing Organisation
LCO	Local Cable Operator
LAN	Local Area Network
MIT	Massachusetts Institute of Technology
MAT	Management Aptitude Test
MIS	Management Information System
MDM	Mid-day Meal
MMP	Mission Mode Project
MW	Medium Wave
MSO	Multi System Operators
MTA	Mid Term Appraisal
NASSCOM	National Association of Software and Services Companies
NeGP	National Employment Guarantee Programme
NGN	Next Generation Networking
NREGA	National Rural Employment Guarantee
NTP	New Telecom Policy

NHRM	National Rural Health Mission
OFC	Optical Fibre Cable
OBC	Other Backward Castes
OBCH	Other Backward Caste High Income
OBCH	Other Backward Caste Medium Income
OBCH	Other Backward Caste Low Income
OLPC	One Laptop Per Child
PCO	Public Call office
PPP	Public Private Partnership
PSU	Public Sector Undertaking
PMO	Prime Minister's Office
PMGSY	Pradhanmantri Gram Sadak Yojana
PKI	Public Key Infrastructure
R&D	Research and Development
RCP	Rural Content Provider
RFID	Radio Frequency Identification
RCP	Rural Community Phones
RF	Radio Frequency
SAT	Scholastic Aptitude Test
SME	Small and Marginal Enterprises
STP	Software Technology Park
SEZ	Special Economic Zone
SSA	Serve Siksha Abhiyan
SWAN	State Wide Area Networks
SW	Short Waves
STB	Set-Top Box
SC	Scheduled Caste
ST	Scheduled Tribe
SCH	Scheduled Caste High Income
SCM	Scheduled Caste Medium Income
SCL	Scheduled Caste Low Income
3GServices	Third Generation Services

TETC	Telecom Testing & Security Certification
TRAI	Telecom Regulatory Authority of India
UIDP	Unique ID Project
USO	Universal Services Obligation
VPT	Village Public Telephones
VoIP	Voice Over Internet Protocol
VSAT	Very small aperture terminals
WiMAX	World Wide Interoperability Micro Wave Access
WiFi	Wireless Fidelity
WLL	Wireless in Local Loop
xDSL	Digital Subscriber Line

Contents

1

Beyond Global Divide

The development equity issue captured in the vogue phrase *digital divide* refers mainly to the global digital scenario. It is limited to digital development disparity between the advanced and the developing countries, and regional development inequalities, at the most, within a country. But India, with large segments of her population crippled with serious social and spatial handicaps, needs understanding the likely impact of digital technology on socio-economic inequalities. Comprehending equity issues at this stage is a policy imperative considering the fast changing techno-economic and social landscape of the world. The digital technology induced-growth in information communication technology (ICT) is reshaping the world economy, and its vibrations are already audible in Indian information communication technology fields.

Why this digital inequality question at all? The answer lies in the fact that the Indian socio-economic fabric is ridden with sharp inequalities, making it more prone to forces like digital technological convergence. Socio-economic equity issues pertaining to information technology development have to be resolved for ensuring equitable future digitalisation and technology convergence initiatives. The concern here is an inclusive digital development. Since the planner's understanding of social equity implications of an otherwise vigorous digital economy is very little at present, this aspect requires serious focus.

The digital-technology-driven growth in information technology (IT) sector and its ubiquitous application in all fields of an economy needs to be examined for its equity aspects from three angles: (a) content and the extent of global digitisation and technological convergence leading to a digital economy; (b) the thrust of the Eleventh Plan Development on bridging the digital-divide; and, (c) understanding the conduciveness of existing socio-economic conditions in moving towards an equitable distribution of digital techno-economic opportunities.

The process of creating content, computing it and communicating it through telephony, cable, satellite and radio in binary digits is called digitisation or digitalisation. This process refers to the shift from the existing analogue technology. In the analogue technology information, audio, visual or data, is captured, computed and communicated in physical quantities, such as weight, voltage or speed. In the digital technology information is captured, computed and communicated in digits representing these physical information.

Convergence of broadcasting and personal computing and communication devices have taken place with the arrival of terrestrial digital broadcasting. This became possible with the invention of Digital TV method, i.e., DigiCipher, in USA in 1990, and beginning of digital broadcasting in 1996 under communication satellite. Classic use of digital convergence lies in one's taking a still or video picture with a digital camera or mobile, and all the possibilities and modes of further customisation and use with the IT and IT-enabled services. Beginning with this thrilling experience of shooting high-quality pictures like a professional photographer, one can feast on a long chain of digital technology benefits. Without waiting for the darkroom process for developing the negative and printing it, one can see the picture on the LCD or a computer monitor. One can edit the picture on one's laptop or PC with a simple software, and send the picture through email or CD or DVD to one's friends or to a studio for high-quality print, or mail it to the news and entertainment media for some fee or voluntarily. One can make use of these pictures in presentations, documents or documentaries. This exemplifies how the traditional boundaries between the producers and the consumers, between professionals and the laymen, and between the information creators and the users, the distributors and the end users, have blurred. The consumer (user) of a camera manufacturing firm, the photo-studio, the film and documentary makers, the courier services for transporting a printing picture, has been enabled to see his camera's end result without involving any of the unavoidable chains of service providers. It does not stop here; he can further edit his capture, send it to others, and generate content (a picture, a document). From an economist's point of view this leads to a long chain of further activities involving sophisticated IT and IT-enabled electronics and services, adding to both income and employment. The levels of economic or other activities have shot up several times as compared to the old analogue technology. The picture from an analogue camera would have needed one to take the film rolls to the studio for developing and keep it in an album. The digital technology by its convergence features spirals physical, mental and creative activities that add to economic gains in one form or another.

1.1. The Digitisation Agenda

Now, as information technology has cast its wondrous spell, the entire world is taking it as a challenge to enter the digital zone. Every country has set a target for a complete shift to the digital mode. This requires massive investment, replacement of the long established information, communication and telecommunication infrastructure, establishing digital production facilities, monitoring, dissemination and storage facilities, and content generation networks. In a nutshell, from creation and capture of information to delivery to reception of content, and their monitoring and storage, every process and facility has to be made digital technology-compatible.

This issue, however, is related to the government's information and communication technology sectors. The importance of the government's programme for digitisation and switchover to digital technology in its information, communication and telecommunication sectors has immediate relevance to overall digital economy, including the private sector. The private sector's dependence on the public sector infrastructure and resources in various forms of cooperation and joint functioning with the government was always there. But in recent times, the governments policy to pool public and private resources for better resource utilisation, making more resource available, and ensuring better service delivery in welfare schemes, faster development of infrastructure, has gained popularity. Since the private sector communication, information, entertainment and publication have more or less gone digital, the government has to follow the suit as a major player with gigantic work.

The content regime includes all that modern men and women need for their entertainment, day-to-day needs, professions, education, etc. This includes a long list of activities and interests: entertainment, publishing, education and data storage. The next stage of digitisation is to make the entire computing realm digital compatible. Computers, computer software and services have to be digital-enabled. The most important, however, is the communications set-up, such as telephony, cable, satellite, radio, and the spectrum.

These threefold regimen not only make the emerging digital economy one of the fastest growing sectors of an economy, but also establishes it as a major growth imperative.

1.2. Inequality Issues

Despite the strong emergence of the IT sector in India's economy, the impact of its growth may not be visible beyond the immediate IT sector and the eligible segments of Indian population with high qualifications and more conducive conditions. In this situation, it may be more relevant to study preparedness of various social and spatial groups in harvesting the new economy crops.

The rationale for studying preparedness lies in the planner's quest to curb any further sharpening of the existing socio-economic disparities on account of information asymmetry. Benefits of information-technology, if left to its natural course of flow, may take ages before the last man in the society realises them. He is crippled with all imaginable handicaps. A poor illiterate villager, an inhabitant of remote forests, deserts or high mountains, or a suburban or urban slum dweller, is nowhere near meeting preconditions for enjoying IT-technology and the digital world boons. His circumstances deprive him of the wealth and development opportunities rising in the new world economy.

The planner, therefore, must know how the existing socio-economic and geographical disadvantages would act upon the percolation of digital economy and society benefits. Apparently, employment and income generation benefits of the accessibility to information network have equalising impacts on the entire society. But in reality, the deciding factors are literacy, income and socio-geographical locations which are going to hamper the flow of digital economy's fruits.

1.3. The Enormity of Inequality

The dimensions of these inequalities are enormous and anomalous. Compare the SC's and the OBC's literacy and poverty status with that of the general category. The comparison is limited to these two reserve categories in view of their predominance in the population of Delhi, which I have studied as a case.

The literacy rates of the SC and the OBC's communities still remain very low as compared to the rest of the population. According to the 2001 census the literacy population of the SC category was 54.69 per cent as compared to the general literacy figure of 64.8 per cent. The female literacy in the SCs was as low as 41.90 per cent as compared to 53.7 per cent of the general literacy. The seriousness of the situation doubles when one goes beyond average literacy rates. Think of the literacy rates of the SC communities in the far flung hills, deserts and forests, and slow improvement evident in decadal literacy rates, showing that except during 1981-1991 and 1991-2001, the rise in total literacy of the SC category was lower than 5 per cent a decade.

Similar is the position of the OBC's and the male-female literacy break up. The regional disparity in their case is as serious as in the case of the SC's. At still another level one's very birth in a disadvantaged social strata might make one suffer slow realisation of new economy's fruits due to complete lack of *social-networking resources*.

The Gross Enrolment Rate, an important indicator of the future literacy scene, is as low as 8.77 per cent in the OBC's, and 6.57 per cent for the SC's, and 11% for the general category. The rural-urban disparity is serious in terms of GER: 6.7 per cent and 19.9 per cent, respectively.

The incidence of poverty too is high in the case of the SC's and the OBC in general as compared to the rest of the population. The below-poverty-line population is 47.3 per cent in the rural ST's population, and 33.3 per cent in the urban ST's population.

This being an approximation of poverty among the weaker sections, the spread of digital economy's benefits among these groups might take long time.

Against this back-drop, first, there is an endeavour to understand digitisation and technological convergence as a major factor responsible for the birth of digital economy. Issues such as what is the nature and scope of digital technology and major emerging themes in the digital economy are discussed. Second, the book would provide a brief coverage on India's digital economy. Third, the nature of the socio-economic inequality issues is discussed. This would endeavour to look into the issues of ill-preparedness of certain sections of the society for plunging into digital economy waves. Fourth, the 11th Plan Agenda for digitalisation and technological convergence and efforts for inclusive growth is examined. Finally, a case study of Delhi that I made as part of my postgraduate course in Pubic Administration in 2007-8 from Indian Institute of Public Administration, New Delhi, is discussed. This case study, backed by 100 sample households survey, throws light on the socio-economic and spatial picture of preparedness to ride on the digital economy waves.

Literature available on these issues was studied. The literature included various works focusing on digital divide experience of the world, and developmental issues and agenda of current Indian planning such as, *Digital Divide* by Mitshuhiro Kagami and Masatsugu Tsuji; *The Emerging Digital Economy* by B. Johansson; *Computer Networks and Internets* by Douglas E. Comer; *IT Experience in India* by Kenneth Keniston and Deepak Kumar; *The New Realities* by Peter F. Drucker; *Why Social Justice Matters*, by Brian Barry.

The works and documents studied for an insight into current Indian plan strategy and investment included: *India Vision 2020; Approach Paper of the 11th Plan; 11th Five Year Plan Document*, Working Group and Steering Committee Reports and Documents of Ministry of Information Technology, Telecommunication, Information and Broadcasting, Human Resource, Health and Family Welfare, and Agriculture and its Allied Sectors.

The book leads gradually from understanding the basic concepts of digitisation and emergence of digital economy, and related issues to gathering insight into planning strategy, and finally examines the socio-economic and spatial strata-wise digital-conduciveness of people through field study survey carried out in Delhi as a case study.

The study of digitalisation and technological convergence, which is the core of ICT sector economics, leads the reader through the labyrinth of technical concepts, the ideas of analogue and digital technology for acquainting with the macro-economic aspects of digitalisation and technological convergence.

The book then imparts an understanding of the technical and technological aspects of ICT and digitalisation, digital economy's structure, problems, challenges and themes concerning or gauging the impact of ICT on the socio-economic fabric of India.

In plowing through India's ICT sector planning and the issues of digital economy, the main concern is probing into the policy issues and initiatives focusing on the socio-economic and geographic equity aspects—such issues as what the government policy had been toward ensuring an egalitarian ICT world in the digital economy age. The main focus here was on the churning that had been going in the Eleventh Plan finalisation process. The Working Group and the Steering Committee Reports and their Recommendations relating to IT, Telecommunication, and Information and Broadcasting sectors, were studied to understand concerns of the stake-holders, including the government, business and industry toward timebound digitalisation with due care to equity and growth concerns with respect to various spatial and social strata.

The next step was to study to what extent digital and IT wonders have touched people's life beyond the high-tech information and communication technology. For this, apart from studying literature and data available, I felt it necessary to dig deeper into the reality through a field survey. For this a field survey of 100 families was conducted.

After understanding how the socio-economic and spatial inequalities influence the spread and percolation pattern of benefits among the people, it was possible to suggest measures for ensuring more equitable development. Why policy measures for equitable development in the digital world? Whatever is the logic of the massive political agenda in this direction, turning the largest number of Indian human resource into productive capital, perhaps, is the largest justification. And for such a goal even the costliest policy is justified.

Developmental impact of uneven spread of information and communication technology and digital economy's fruits among various socio-economic and socio-geographic segments may be far more damaging than the Ancient Indian society's act of denying the less privileged an access to Sanskrit script. Just as denial of literacy to people from the disadvantaged social strata and locations in the past had made them stagnate for centuries so letting today's information superhighway train leave them behind may cost the society dearly.

1.4. Objectives

The focus of the book is on understanding the process and pace of digitalisation and converging technology in the Indian scenario. In this I aimed at gaining an insight into the national agenda for going digital at the earliest so that the country was able to keep pace with the rest of the world, and cash in on its IT strength. In this the *Vision 2020,* and *ICE Committee Sub-Group Reports, Going Digital,* and *The Spectrum,* were discussed. Finally, the 11th Plan scenario, as emerging from the plan debate, and various Working Group and Steering Committee, were discussed to decide the path ahead.

The purpose of this book is to highlight the metamorphosis that information technology has brought about in content creation, computing, communication, and delivery and reception in the field of information and broadcasting, publication, entertainment, business, governance, health and lifestyle. The ways in which information is spread and accessed, and the entertainment industry works, and humans entertain themselves; and the ways in which education takes place have further empowered those with better education, abundance of wealth, and equipped them with the latest in technological wonders. The most pivotal factor adding to one's business and economic strength is information. Information asymmetry is one of the major reasons for growth and development differential in various economic activities. Individuals, societies and firms with access to faster channels of data tend to make advance on the others. In fact this, imperfection in knowledge of a thing, alone makes it possible for the business and industry to thrive on profits.

Another major objective is to understand how information asymmetry dims the prospectus of higher income and employment among the disadvantaged strata of Indian society. The idea is based on the historical perception that traditional middle-men-dominated economies existed because the middlemen knew markets, had means to reach there, and sell what the producers of an industrial, agriculture and arts and crafts goods produced. Information-asymmetry, the producers' ignorance about the buyers, and buyers' unawareness of the best sources, similar situations of imperfect knowledge in demand and supply of goods and services and opportunities, led to severe socio-economic inequalities and empowered exploitative machines. In earlier times, the information-disabilities of those living in far-off, isolated regions, and of those living in the pockets of social backwardness were far less.

In the past literacy was the major bar. But with respect to Information, Communication and Technology (ICT)-enabled-information, the disabilities are several and formidable. Added to illiteracy are now economic inability to buy expensive computing and receiving facilities, the non-availability of communication networks, and the unaffordability to have access to content.

This raises the issue whether the ICT growth in Indian economy so far has reached the less educated, the poor and socio-economically and geographically disadvantaged lots? What would be the impact of these ICT sector growth on the already existing inequalities when the country along with the rest of the world will step in a fully digital world in coming decades?

This can be understood by gauging the development effect of IT and IT-enabled services on various socio-economic and spatial group's; or by seeing the manifestation of benefits of this sector among various strata. The first would require studying the socio-economic strata-wise ownership of firms, share in employment, and income generation, professional and educational qualifications targeting opportunities in the digital economy.

The second approach is basing the study on manifestation of benefits in terms of conduciveness of the population to a shift to digital economy and society, or its amenability to make good of the digital economy opportunity.

I found the second approach appropriate for several reasons. First, since the IT and IT-enabled services, as important expressions of digital economy, are yet to emerge in their full strength to make any visible impact on socio-economic equality. Second, amenability of individuals to emerging opportunities in the digital age is easy to be gauged from simple verifiable facts, such as, computing paraphernalia, communication connectivity, content use pattern, and people's future perception of IT and IT-enabled services, and the entire digital economy. Third, the focus of the book being futuristic, I am more concerned with studying the present indicators to understand the impact of digital technology on the future socio-economic status of the disadvantaged lot.

2

Global Digital Economy

What is a digital world economy, and what are the major issues related to it? These are questions that would be answered in this section. New Technology means a shift from analogue to digital one, and change from semiconductors to microprocessors, from host to client or server computing, from bandwidth to information highway, from data and text to voice, image and multimedia, from dumb to intelligent networks. All these information technology changes are being further responded to by business and industry. It is this interface between information communication technology and business which gave birth to digital economy, the new world economy.

2.1. The Global Economy Themes

A Digital Economy, as it emerges from literature, and the functioning of IT, Telecommunication, and Information and Broadcasting sectors of the world, flourishes on certain ubiquitous new themes transforming the economy.

Knowledge-Based Solutions

Knowledge-centric solutions to economic problems of production, marketing, advertising, consumption and management, and other problems of modern society, have become the mantras. The presence and component of knowledge in goods and services have increased phenomenally. Production processes, packaging, distribution and consumption of goods and services, and infrastructural facilities, household and institutional management, security and vigilance, everything has acquired IT wisdom.

Smart clothes with manufacturing information chips, smart cards of various shades, such as smart houses fitted with IT-based security and remote control, smart roads capable of sensing traffic and weather conditions to reduce accidents, smart cards, smart tyres, smart radio and television have become the order of the day in the new knowledge economy.

The technology challenge has increased seriously due to the involvement of knowledge technology, expert system, artificial intelligence.

2.2. From Analogue to Digitisation

Digital content creation, storage and transmission has threefold advantage over the analogue one: high content quality with high definition television compatibility, high quality transmission and reception, and compressibility of data enabling much higher transmission on a given spectrum. These three features have metamorphosed the economics of the information technology, telecommunication and information and broadcasting media units. It has made possible multifarious use of content, revolutionary savings on spectrum costs, and sparing information and broadcasting media units of government and private sector of the crushing burden of terrestrial transmission networks.

This triggered the digitalisaiton race in every sector of the economy, and a policy of fast shift in technology, skills and content towards a complete digital world economic order in every country. Though the changing facet of technology is the real determinant, faster development of many advanced countries in digital technology, and their focus on complete shift from analogue to digital technology in every respect is one major concern. The entire gamut of socio-economic and commercial activities have come on digits, and the technology is fast moving to the digital one. All media units are headed to be completely digitalised.

This requires that every economy follow suit to keep pace to be compatible with the rest of the world. This means a fast shift to the digital mode in the fields of information technology, telecommunication, and information and broadcasting.

The Virtual Solutions

Virtualisation of a large number of economic and other activities has taken place, wherein the physical presence of a person or a set-up or a thing is not required for performing an action on the targeted object or person. Virtual aliens, i.e., BPO workers, virtual ballot boxes, virtual business parks, virtual congress, i.e., legislative hearings held from multiple locations, an asynchronously (multiple time dimension), and dozens of other activities have their virtual avatars.

This has overcome the resource mobilisation constraints in many ways. Depending on their own resource position, various firms now go for solutions that can overcome their acute labour scarcity and high wage problems by going for BPO or KPO solutions, or operating from less developed markets.

Molecular Operational Scale

The idea of molecularisation tells of the new world economy's finding that solutions to the mass-driven, traditional hierarchical corporate bodies lie in enabling them to disaggregate into their molecules, i.e., the knowledge workers, clusters of individual entrepreneurs. These molecules bound by business interest (as electrical force in a substance) may acquire the traits of a solid or a liquid – either making it impossible for the molecules to move within the substance, or too loose to be able to maintain a structure. The new world economy needs the liquid crystal property of allowing both adequate structural bonding and mobility to its molecules.

This became possible as the digital world with information super highway provided answers to the 1991 Nobel Laureate Ronald Coase's question why a group of individuals work under one organisation. Since with the internetworking the time and money cost of acquiring information regarding production processes, finance, markets and management have come down significantly, the seamless possibility of an individual being simultaneously both consumer and producer, and both buyer and seller has been realised.

Internetworking enables corporate and other organisations to carry out their business through networking. This opens up the possibility of IT and IT-enabled services of BPO and KPO, and other ways of solving resource and knowledge constraints by virtual approach.

Disintermediation

Business in the pre-knowledge world was possible only with large intermediary set-ups facilitating the matching interest of the producers and consumers. These included agents, wholesalers, distributors, retailers and brokers or middle managers. There was an entire business segment handling these activities grouped as execution of business transaction. They flourished in a world of imperfect information, distances, and lack of means for choosing things, or doing things, without physically being present. But the scene changed with the arrival of digital technology of enabling one to get voice, image and data available to you on the net. This brought the producers and service providers face to face with the end users or consumers. This in one stroke left the intermediaries redundant.

The near cost-free availability of, and access to, all kinds of information has reduced the barriers to information and cost. Disintermediation has sped up the process of delivery, improved the interaction between the producers of goods and service. All this has led to higher efficiency levels in production, distribution and management, wages and profits.

Business firms and organisations engaged in production and distribution of goods and services, politics, governance and civil society—every type of organisation is feeling the power of getting close to its target population. The advantages are enormous. In the very process of interacting with their customers, clients, now a firm builds rich data, and the customer literally participates in the process of improvement of the firm's products, and ways of delivery and packaging. The seller of a good or service has become an information buyer vis-à-vis his customer. Most importantly, they are now just-a-click away, making possible extreme customisation of production, and delivery.

This had a metamorphosing impact on the ways producers sell their stuff to the consumers with lesser dependence on the retail business giants, the way hoteliers and tourist resort owners marketed their services to the tourists, the way educational institutions interacted with their aspirant students for enrolment, the way the local grocers and restaurants deliver their stuff to the customers, and the way the commercial real estate brokers have to change their ways.

Another major field where disintermediation was felt is governance. Being the largest single body interacting with the public from a multitude of departments and ministries in an almost one way, archetypical hierarchical fashion, the government now can directly deal with its subjects in more time-saving, faster and economical ways. In the field of politics and civil society activities, the way and means of mobilising people, discussing issues, and gathering public opinion and letting the common men know the party view or the causes of a civil society group have become a different game altogether. It has become extremely fast, effective, time and energy saving, more of an interactive and twosome game.

Convergence

Technological convergence, as a direct outcome of the shift of information technology from analogue to digital mode, has encompassed information, communication and telecommunication directly, changing the way humans live, communicate, do business, entertain, manage office and home, carry out research and development, and think.

Technological convergence in its digital economy avatar has moved three sectors of activities: (a) computing and computation-related activities of computer hardware, software, application systems, all gadgets and accessories related to these; (b) communication and communication-related goods and services, such as transmitters, other transmission-related equipments, uplinking and downlinking equipments and facilities; (c) content creation activities, digitalisation of old analogue content wealth, diversification of content regime by focusing on interactive gaming, and cartoon movies. The corporate vision of these sectors may differ, but the emerging dominant view is that just as the automotive industry has dominated the entire world economy earlier so digital technology is going to remain the main sector of the future economies.

Innovation

Innovation has always been the key to leadership in every

industry at every stage of development. But this has acquired a new dimension in the digital economy's technological convergence age. Now instead of waiting for the market and the technology indicating obsolescence, the developers of a technology, a product, or a service, target to obsolete its latest and the best by replacing them by one with more innovative features. Take the case of Microsoft replacing its DOS with Windows, and the endless new versions of Microsoft Windows being introduced before the market declares its products obsolete.

This may be in response to the pressing need for continuing one's leadership in the market, but largely it is due to fast technological innovations taking place in every field, and the availability of information-related services as data on consumers's or users' taste and requirement, the developments in related areas of research and development, and easy networking for conferences, funding and patents.

In a digital world innovations, rewarding innovators, finding fund supports, investors and all other related services have got better internet-worked.

Prosumption

Prosumption means endless refinement of products and services with inclusion of more knowledge content, more customisation, and reshaping products to meet the consumer's needs from all angles, and keeping the producers fed with all inputs that users can provide expressing their needs.

The gap between consumers and producers have vanished, and consumer information and technology have become producers by human collaboration on the net. This phenomenon is true of not only manufactures-consumers relationship, but also of the manufacture-manufacturing equipment/services relationship wherein the equipment and service suppliers become sellers or producers, and the manufacturers take the place of the buyers or customers.

Extreme customisation of goods and services in design, delivery and maintenance, and related services have become possible with information superhighway-enabled perfect interaction between all sets of produces of goods and services across all the chains of producers and consumers, sellers and buyers, distributors/wholesalers and retailers. Like a customer sitting in a restaurant with his stuff served from a table-top kitchen set to cook and spice his food to his taste, you can do the virtual assembling and designing of your own car out of the list of parts, get done virtual test-drive, and get the car delivered at a short notice.

Immediacy

Earlier it used to take long time to conceive an idea, formulate a plan to execute it, execute the plan to give it a finished product or service shape, and get it in the market. But now in the IT and IT-enabled scenario of business and industry, this entire process is completed in a year or two even in an automotive industry. Immediacy is the hallmark of today's economy. The business and industry metabolism has heightened. There is a real time data and information exchange between the producers and consumers, between the distributors and retailers, between the research and development and marketing wings of a firm. The time and cost of reaching crucial data and resources have reduced substantially. The time gap between arrival and off-take of supply consignments have reached just-on-time standards.

Globalisation

Contrary to MIT professor Paul Krugman's view (in his book *Peddling and Prosperity*) that there is nothing more to the global economy than trade in goods, services, capital, labour and information, today's knowledge-driven world economy was never so global in its character even while allowing the national, regional and local individuality of operation.

The compelling need for being competent to meet global standards, global taste, global fashion, global art-of-living, global new age knowledge has led to a larger degree of globalisation. This trend can be seen more evidently in the increasing trends of free-trade zones, group-versus-group competition. From an individual country's stand point, globalisation is both the driver and the driven.

In the IT and ICT-dominated world all social, economic, cultural activities have lost their time and space meaning. To this extent, every firm in the national economy has to understand the need for being compatible with the rest of the world in all respects of digital technology to be operating on time, on line, and on real time basis.

Discordance

Discordance is the negative theme that policy makers, project managers and funding agencies have to be cautious about whenever an economic development project, a development concept, a production or marketing process, or pricing of a product, or factors of production is under consideration.

These issues emerged at the departing point between the old and new economies. There are three issues mainly. First, an economy in the move from analogue to digital mode faces the problems of large-scale laying off of the old regime skilled workers leaving them to suffer joblessness or miserably low pay packets, while the new economy knowledge workers get unheard pay packages and living extravagant life. Second, the organisational pressure on the employees have increased tremendously to perform and identify themselves with the firm, but without any share in the fast-multiplying wealth. Third, on the technology front, the problems are equally serious. Contrasting computing architecture, competing standards, legacy systems vis-à-vis new technology paradigm are the problems being faced in the global economies.

But the real stakes of the civilisation as it moves towards digital domain have to do with unpredictability of technology's impacts on humans and all living beings on biological, social and environment levels, and their repercussion on economic well-being. Graham Bell's invention of telephone meant for the deaf turned out to be more of a commercial revolution in communication than human well being; Einstein's theory of relativity mushroomed destructive weapons, the wonderful motor car choked the cities.

The excellence of digital technology meant intrusion of electronic gadgets in the mental and social life, increasing human dependence, for all kinds of mental and physical activity, on digital devices and equipments. This, in the first place, might in the long run numb the human mind, reducing the average human mental capability in calculation, working out simple things, and disabling the use of the mind's fertile endowments. Second, worse, the connivance of technology and market-determinism confounds the human ability to guide their tools to act in responsible and desirable ways. It is in this context that the twin principles of responsible technology use and responsible corporate investment criteria are needed to be ensured by effective regulation of every proposal aiming for commercial exploitation of a technological invention. The most feared aspect of internet technology, however, was the invasion of individual privacy. This fear was partially true, but with effective regulatory measures, this seems to be controllable.

2.3. The Internet-worked Economy

Information technology on its surface looks like a technology that does not go beyond facilitating flow of information, speeding up MIS, and making fast online communication possible within organisations and among organisations. Sending an email, voice mail or conducting an audio-visual conference appears to be the only fruits of IT. But in reality there is much more than this to the world of information technology. There is an entire world of innovative ways to revolutionising business by using IT.

The focus here is to create business. Don Tapscott, in his book *Digital Economy,* talked of how five layers of internetworked structures lead to business transformation. This strategy goes beyond the conventional focus on improving quality, cost-reduction and business-process reengineering, and human imperative. The traditional ways of business and industry was more driven by the new technologies and managerial invention focusing on reducing costs of productions and management and distribution.

Internetworking shifted the focus to business transformation and business creation. This transformation process is multi-layered. The first layer formed of an individual equipped with personal multi-media and assigned with the task of learning efficiency. This liberated the individual worker from conventional print and computation-oriented island of operation with little dynamism and collaboration with the outside world. The multimedia, with its voice, image and data connectivity online within and without the organisation, and placed on the international information superhighway, enables the individual to act and access faster, to source information, update oneself, to seek advice, and test an idea or concept promptly.

The effective individual is guided by a high performance team. This team, equipped with work-group computing facilities and assigned with the task of business process and job redesign, basically enables the firms to respond quickly to business environment and increasing customer demands. It brings skilled people, finance and other resources together. It replaces the old system of islands of technology interacting with old bureaucratic structures. This is the result of the new media-generated possibility of collaborative knowledge work through high capacity, ever-changing, open networked teams. These teams are free from linear control models, and, instead of the individual to manager accountability model, follows the server-service-unit to the client model. As an improvement upon the successful Japanese technology-enabled team leader approach in the automobile industry, the American manufacturer's workgroup approach was based on technology. Whereas the team approach under a powerful technology-enabled leader had all high-performing individuals from various related fields in the team, the workgroup approach used technology as a base for collaborating with all related services and resource providers using the powers of the new media. The workgroup approach used concurrent working instead of serial, which produced better synergy. For example, when work on a machine project begins, just the criteria are explained to a designer workgroup, the designers collaborate around with work stations online, the designs is conceived, the machine is assembled and put on tests in all conditions online on the computer monitor, before the real work starts. Boeing 777 is an example of such workgroup-based designing, supply of parts from different producers, assembling and testing, and finally getting delivered.

The next layer of internetworked business is integrated organisation. Here, unlike business reengineering processes, which are inventions of technologists, and face legacy technologies, in integrated business the focus is on enterprise infostructure: business, applications, information and technology. Equipped and facilitated with enterprise infostructure, its focus is on organisational transformation. This frees business and industry from hierarchy because with the enterprise infostructure, access to information is free and wide. There is a worldwide corporate cohesiveness with the strong media and information superhighway available now. This concept frees the enterprise from seeing profit as a price differential, and highlights the approach of creating wealth by value additions. Everything is done by partnering than staffing.

The fourth layer of internetworked business is extended enterprise. This is equipped with enterprise infostructure, and its objective is recasting external relationships. Just as in the integrated enterprise the physical and other distances vanish due to infostructure, so do these disappear in the extended enterprise. Now here the enterprises interact with outside organisations and their access to all related information being generated by various related firms across the value addition chains. Enterprise computing enables firms to share crucial information regarding one's own entity and those of the others. This has led the corporation towards virtual corporates, with a huge portion of total transaction being handled virtually. This virtualisation of transactions means not only huge operational cost cuts, time savings and effectiveness, but also value chain creation. The value chains lead to value network, and value network means value generation due to technology.

New economic dynamics have emerged out of interenterprise computing. These are: accessibility of partners, new interdependencies, faster inter-organisational metabolism, more cooperative competitiveness, and rapid interorganisational value creation.

The topmost layer in the internetworked business is characterised by its worldwide connectivity through net and focus on wealth creation and social development. Empowered by the internet's world wide web of information, and founded on the layers of effective individuals, high performance team, and the integrated enterprise, the firm is now able to create wealth. This amounts to getting on the I-Way by creating a cluster of virtual firms corresponding to each step or process, or item of work, and beginning the action.

2.4. News Media and Entertainment

One of the important fields of knowledge economy was publishing. This sector, ever since the invention of the printing press, has been moving on in the old lines of production processes, packaging, marketing and economics. With the arrival of IT technology and internetworking, and accessibility of information on all required aspects, from manuscript preparation to editing, printing and publishing available to an individual, and the possibility of deviating from the print run economics, now the publishing scenario has changed. Not only this, even e-publishing of books, journals, and newspapers has become a reality.

With the digitalisation of technology, the information and broadcasting scenario has completely changed. The most important effect is in terms of high-quality transmission of audio and visual content through both the radio and the television media. Not only this, digital technology enables broadcasting to go high definition in its visual segments, meaning that a rich interactive television would now be possible. Another aspect of this change due to digitalisation is the multiple use of every piece of information/content generated. These features of digital technology make it possible to put broadcasting contents to more than one use.

The best feature of digital technology, however, lies in compression of data and information so that very little bandwidth is consumed. Since bandwidth is a scarce and expensive facility, this means substantial reduction in broadcasting cost.

But for a country like India, the real challenge lies in shifting to digital broadcasting in the shortest possible time so that it can keep pace with the rest of the world. This would need the planners to look into mainly two sets of things: the phasing out of the existing analogue transmitters by simulcasting digital transmitters for a short transition period, and then complete switchover to the digital mode. The real concern here would be completing the task in the shortest optimum period, while minimising simulcasting costs.

Since digitalisation means generation of additional economic activities through value addition to existing activities, and also repurposing them, both income and employment generation possibilities in a digitalised broadcasting scenario goes up significantly. With the opening of new value addition activities, new employment opportunities also will emerge.

The internetworking, and the increasing number of internet users and increasing number of daily need transaction, all indicate the possibility of increasing the scope of making information available to the netizens on the wings of audio visual advertisements. Every information or content worth any use or interest to even the smallest segments of the surfing people would be made available on the information superhighway for free use by the internet users. This means a wonderful scenario of having all relevant information available on the net just a click away, for use to the best of one's abilities, and that too in return for viewing mind-blowing advertisements.

Gaming is another important segment of the digital IT world. This means availability of all kinds of high-quality games with the highest image and voice features. Considering the growing number of digital age young population, born and brought up online, the scope for gaming content production, making them available on the internet on various terms of use, is phenomenal. This sector needs utmost priority among the digital economy activities. Since to meet the demand for a large number of users, gaming contents would be required to be produced on the large scale, and at every stage, from conception of the idea to finally placing a game on different modes of marketing, a large number of skilled manpower would be required. This will open up huge opportunities of employment and income.

2.5. Internetworked Governance and Learning

The internetworked health systems for perfect functioning of health-care services by enabling expertise and facilities reach in the remotest corners without having to bringing patients and the physicians together at one place physically. This is an example of how internet and IT technology can resolve many social service sector problems of an economy.

Similarly, now the governments equipped with the internetworking systems connecting various organs of the government among themselves and with the citizens can maintain continuous online linkage for faster action and improvement, quicker feedback and response.

The learning process is the greatest beneficiary of internetworking. Work and learning have become the same, and learning has become a challenge as it has shifted away from schools and universities to digits, and learning institutions are reinventing themselves by opening up online courses, and creating infostructure in their own premises, and providing cyberspace tutors.

2.6. New Economy Issues

The new economy, however, has its own shares of problems and typical issues.

Employment and Jobs

1. The larger firms and government entities are moving towards downsizing of their clerical as well as professional and managerial staff in response to the concepts of molecularisation and knowledge-centric management.
2. Even though the cumulative effect of convergence of computing, communication and content, and the enormous growth in small and medium-size companies will raise employment and income opportunities, the technological shift required for the same is likely to cause transitional pains.
3. The developing countries are on the way to experiencing a rush of global big players sensing that they may grow at a higher rate in these countries than their own developed economy environment.
4. There is, and would be, a simultaneous upsurge in high-paying special-skill jobs, and also in lower-paying jobs in service countries, while old economy jobs will decline significantly.
5. As a result of internetworking business, which de-links work from the physical presence of the workers, the pattern of physical location of workforce vis-à-vis individual

workers, vis-à-vis the clients, and the employers has undergone a serious change, which would further reduce social intercourse and harmony in a workplace.

Access and Equity

The main issue that concerns digital economy is access to and equity in information technology wonder. These issues, though equally relevant to even the most advanced countries, are of more significance to developing countries like India. What will be the ramifications of sharp disparities in access to these new economy wonders due to various age old disabilities. These disabilities include socio-economic and spatial disadvantages, and also learning attainments of individual from various backgrounds.

Quality of Life

In the new economy, due to the shift to knowledge work, fast vanishing of concepts of job for life and a career, the lifestyle is changing. People are facing issues of compensations, income and equitable social distribution system of benefit of economy. The equity and distribution of benefits become important issues as the means of production are increasingly orienting to the mind's power of knowledge. The worst is that nothing inherent in the new technology is likely to improve the quality of life.

Electronic Democracy and Polity

An interactive internetworking for representation in a political system, or reorganisation of different interest groups on an issue, or disintermediation of the conventional political agents for mobilising public opinion or action on some issue has already started showing results in the present system.

Macro-economy and the Nation State

The major issue here is to decide as to who is responsible to society's transformation. The various views being aired by academicians and thinkers range from the faith in the market mechanism perfection in letting benefits flow to the last man in the society to holding a corporate sector responsible for societal share of growth and benefits, the civil society and non-governmental organisations rising to its societal responsibilities, and, finally, leaving it to the government intervention.

But a thoughtful look at various opinions would make it clear that the corporate sector, the civil society, and the government have to get together to ensure society's welfare in terms of lessening transition pains, and ensuring social nets for securing social safety.

3

India's Digital Agenda

The information and communication technology sector (ICT) in India has drawn national and global attention due to its spectacular growth, and its role as a development stimuli in a wide range of social and economic sectors. Though directly linked to information, broadcasting and telecommunication, information technology (IT) has become the focal point for development of the entire gamut of technology development and research. Everything that is invented and evolved in the world of computing, communications, and computer software and contents, widens the scope and level of economic activities. Beyond these, then, are all those sectors which find computer and internet solutions feasible in their activities. IT applications, thought to be limited to a few sectors at the beginning of the IT revolution, now cover solutions to almost every economic and social activity. Why is ICT playing so vital a role in development? The answer lies in the fact that like any infrastructure, ICT fulfils the basic condition for development and promotion of various sectors of an economy today. The new world economy cannot be imagined without the ICT infrastructure in place. The economies of various countries have already become digital. There is no economic sector that can strive to grow at a higher pace without digitalising itself.

The importance of IT in today's Indian economy is so much that since the Eleventh Plan the Union Plan Planning Commission made it bounden on every Union and State Ministry and Department to allocate 2 per cent of the total budget outlay on IT and related activities. Though accepted with some scepticism, it came out later that many laudable developments took place. Not only the obvious IT beneficiary economic sectors of telecommunication, postal services, information and broadcasting, but also information technology is transforming all shades of economic, scientific and social activities. IT is being widely used in all forms of industrial and managerial activities; all forms of social services sectors such as medicine, health, education, policing; and such sectors as agriculture, fishery and forestry; and science and technology spheres, as in space, meteorology and nanotechnology. In Andhra Pradesh the entire range of agricultural statistics, right from land use statistics to rainfall data, is being gathered online and made available to the policy and decision makers.

India is moving fast towards becoming a digital economy. Already it has earned itself the status of prized IT and IT-enabled services outsourcing destination. Beginning with high priority to IT during the 10th Plan, the goals during the Eleventh Plan is much more ambitious.

But the purpose of going through the plan agenda of the government during the Eleventh Plan is to examine the policy and plan content aimed at ensuring equitable spread of ICT, and ICT-induced benefits to all segments of the society in the remotest parts of the country, without an adverse effect on the present socio-economic development balance.

3.1. Information Technology

The Eleventh Five Year Plan, as apparent from the final plan document, and the Steering Committee and the Working Group reports and recommendations, underscores the paramount role that information technology has played in global trade and services through productivity benefits of IT technology, and increase in IT-enabled services (ITES). Medical transcriptions, call centres, data processing, back-office operations, Geographical Information System (GIS), revenue accounting, etc., and the new economy providing end-to-end business solutions, system integration, remote management, etc., are acknowledged as major areas of economic and social change and growth stimuli.

The Indian economy felt the growth impact in terms of employment and income generation on the one hand, and a rise in direct tax-collection, and the much needed increase in spending rates on the other hand. The massive potential in industrial value creation, and growth strength of India in IT software and services and ITES, and the hard-earned position as the premier global IT and ITES sourcing destination, all call for evermore focus on this sector in the Eleventh Plan. Availability of higher bandwidth and higher version of work-flow management software have increased the scope of this sector all the more.

The multiplicity of service lines and verticals emerging provide a 'make or break' opportunity, and has placed India into a high-growth orbit and on a fast track towards attaining the developed nation status.

The Eleventh Plan documents place IT and IT-enabled services in two segments: (i) Exports; and, (ii) Domestic categories: related to R&D and engineering services, consulting services, system integration, application development and maintenance, traditional IT outsourcing, horizontal services; and *verticals* sector of agriculture, banking, insurance, manufacturing, health care and pharmaceuticals, travel and hospitality, animation, media and entertainment, biotechnology and life sciences, nanotechnology, courts and legal, power and energy, VLSI and CAD, automobile and transportation, and, finally, smart governance.

Information Monopoly

A quick probe into the developmental impact of these emerging and already happening fields of development should have made planner the sit up and think as to what it would mean not to enable the large reservoir of its manpower to ride the tides of ITESs. Just a look at the literacy and poverty figures, indicating people likely to remain deprived of boons of IT and ITES's, will be enough to realise the gravity with which equity-related issues need to be taken up in India, lest the already inequality-stricken society push socio-economic inequalities further leading to social conflicts. In the heart of such fears is the world experience of monopoly over information and technology by a handful of people and nations, and the consequent subjugation of entire parts of the world by a few nations, entire societies by a small section. What is more, monopoly over knowledge and information by a few when they have already amassed wealth disproportionately can prove worse.

This can be evermore damaging to the society's welfare and balanced growth when the ground realities for a large proportion of one billion strong nation are averse to any attempt to offer them their part of the cake. Think of the minuscule percentage of Indians who are effectively educated to gain directly and proportionately from IT and ITES's benefited economic activities in the rural or urban areas. The same Andhra Pradesh which is in the forefront of India' IT revolution, whose agriculture sector prides in having an online agriculture statistics gathering and dissemination system, has a farm sector with unprecedented phenomena of farmer-suicides recently. Not only that, its showcased achievement of IT and ITES's development in agriculture may not be of any material meaning to farmers who are illiterate, poverty-stricken, and deprived of all those basic amenities and the knowledge insight which can ensure them their share in this development.

The illiterate small or marginal farmers are now more exposed to fast movement of the bigger farmers and market players who have access to all information related to farming, farm produce marketing, facilities, and changes in prices and policies. Even the simple information about rainfall and other agriculture statistics can be accessed only by farmers who can own a computer and have a compatible literacy. And among farmers too, the farmers from scheduled castes and scheduled tribes, and other backward classes are likely to be much less equipped with education and facilities needed to enjoy these benefits. Therefore, one must look at the policy and issues, reforms and new initiatives being undertaken by the government.

Policy Issues, Reforms and New Initiatives

An examination of the Eleventh Plan documents and the plan discussion that have gone into the planning process would reveal policy lines likely to be followed to ensure equitable development in IT and ITES in the country. The major lines of action suggested in the plan documents are as follows:

1. Promoting the supply of suitable IT talent, in the short-run, by bringing in finishing schools, and finishing programmes to top up the skill levels of graduate students; and bridge-courses for mid-level managers.

2. In the long term, the education system would be expanded rapidly at all levels to include a huge number of Masters and Doctoral programmes, and developing manpower in some of the niche areas like IT in health care, transportation, manufacturing, nanotechnology, animation and entertainment, etc.
3. The need to provide the necessary resources and policy framework for achieving the desired objectives through a joint effort by industry and government has been accepted as a priority.

The main points of concern are:

1. Introduction of standardised national level tests similar to SAT, GRE, AGRE, MAT, etc., for benchmarking of students seeking admissions in undergraduate and postgraduate institutes in India.
2. Rating and accreditation of all educational institutions by an independent agency.
3. Introduction of a common nationwide benchmark for assessing graduating students and inclusion of industry needs in this assessment process.
4. Making the teaching /academics profession more attractive and respectable.
5. Encouraging students and working professionals to pursue further education for skill enhancement.
6. Periodic review and updating of curriculum to make it more industry-oriented and encouraging faculty to constantly upgrade skills.
7. Building adequate basic, business and social infrastructure by strengthening the intra-city road network and public transport infrastructure to decongest existing hubs.
8. Decentralisation of the industry beyond existing hubs by developing new townships.
9. Introduction of faster public transport (high speed trains similar to TGV of France and Bullet of Japan) between important cities.

Another area of priority is ensuring a favourable business policy and regulatory environment with special focus on encouraging SMEs and new ventures by: (i) Continuation of the benefits provided by the STPI scheme, (ii) Strengthening the IP protection, data privacy and information security environment in the country, (iii) providing support for SME segment growth to ensure that SMEs can continue to leverage the benefits offered under the STP / SEZ scheme without constraints on where they may be located, and (iv) Ensuring adequate access to venture capital and angel funding for start-ups.

Global Trade Development and Promotion of Global Free Trade in Services, and fostering a sustainable ecosystem for innovation and R&D need to be ensured by: (a) developing core capabilities at the academic level in identified focus areas; (b) encouraging industry-academia participation in R&D; (c) facilitating the incubation/commercialisation of innovations, (c), and by IPR's awareness.

The transformation of the industry from the BPO-dominated one to knowledge society, i.e., KPO and HR concepts, implies higher levels of activities, and more emphasis on knowledge content based products and concepts, and higher levels of knowledge-based workers with required excellence, which is a bigger challenge than providing goods, and needs higher competitiveness. This would require mechanism for identifying the newly emerging verticals, and generating suitable manpower.

The Software Technology Parks' (STP) success story indicates how a favourable business policy and a regulatory environment critical for any sector and the STP scheme plays a role in moving the economy in the right direction. It had a major impact on placing India on the global map as an IT superpower, and helped resolve growth, foreign exchange, employment generation and the development issues of India. Under the STP scheme, units engaged in the export of IT and ITES are entitled to tax benefits under section 10A and 10B of Income Tax Act 1961, scheduled to lapse in post-assessment year 2009-10.

IT in school education is targeted to be promoted through using ICT tools in classrooms by better monitoring of attendance and performance of the students as well as teachers, using ICT in Management Information Systems (MIS), and monitoring the national projects of Sarva Siksha Abhiyan (SSA), Mid-Day Meal (MDM) and Integrated Child Development Scheme (ICDS), etc.

Gender empowerment through IT and ITES sectors has taken a lead with their large participation in these sectors. In line with the basic principles of governance, a commitment of government, under the National Common Minimum Programme, the government has introduced gender budgeting to support schemes of gender empowerment through ICT for reducing the digital divide. The increased presence of women in the huge US$ 39.6 billion project would break the gender disparity.

The Main IT Faculty Development

For making academics as attractive a career option as an industry professional career, academic institutes need to provide suitable faculty remuneration as there is a large gap between the salary structures in the industry and in the academics. Industry needs to come forward and supplement the government efforts through establishment of Chairs for professors, incentives, sponsored-research and the like, in the following ways:

1. There is a need to increase the number of faculty positions in the Indian universities and technical institutions as well as creation of adjunct faculty from industry to address the twin issue of quantity and quality and R&D activities.
2. There is a need to tie up with institutions abroad for professors to come here on sabbatical.
3. There is a to need to train the ICT faculty of both the formal and the non-formal sector of education to keep pace with the demands of the industry as well as the technological changes.
4. There is a need to develop a mechanism to encourage migration of students between formal and non-formal streams to address the issue of quantity; also to introduce a credit system whereby the students can accumulate and carry forward their credits and complete their education at their own pace. This would particularly help the in-service personnel.
5. There is a need to evolve a National Mission for faculty development in general; and faculty development in such IT-enables services as IT in tourism, health, medical and legal services and finance in particular.

6. The significance of IT in the health sector has been recognised by development of integrated disease surveillance projects, creation of District and State Health Data Centres for the surveillance units, networking and operation of district health centres through video-based distance communications, early warning system for disease incidence and collection of call centre-based information, web-based health management information systems and telemedicine are some of the important areas that need to be operationalised. Electronic health, i.e., e-health, is one of the next frontiers of ICT innovations.

IT in the agriculture sector has been fully launched by identifying agriculture as one of the Mission Mode Projects under the National E-Governance Plan (NEGP), which is a nationwide initiative for promoting e-governance in the country by the Agricultural Resources Information System.

IT Technology in Agriculture

Even agriculture and its allied sectors are focusing on technology for faster and effective development. One important project undertaken during Eleventh Plan is Strengthening and Promoting Agriculture Information System through IT. With an outlay of Rs.350 crore under this scheme the work of modernisation of management of land records would be taken up. This would facilitate the process of registration and mutation by integrating them into the function of deed-registration and the system of land-based public services, such as certification, accessing land records, and making functions of fixing eligibility for development aid and facilities faster and effective.

Also this set of data would be integrated into three layers of data: (a) forest summary, (b) cadastral maps; and (c) revenue records, and harmonise them with Geographical Information System to evolve a comprehensive plan for development, regulation, and disaster management. Computerisation of spatial and textual records and integration of registration office for exploring Torrens' title-based land record rather than the current deed-based system would be a huge step forward.

But the real value-addition would be the arrangement for accessing land records by the farmers as owners of land which needs further facilitation for enabling the farmers in term of acquaintance with computers, setting up computers with connectivity, and making online access possible as it is in bank accounts and lockers.

IT in the rural sector would be promoted by creating *Rural Content Providers (RCPs).* This is envisaged to make the PCs and internet an attractive proposition to a much larger number of people. In this effort the private sector too would be involved, and it would boost and drive the demand for both PCs and Internet access.

Targets of IT-ITES Sector for the Eleventh Five Year Plan

Against the backdrop of large untapped demand potential and strong fundamentals, India is uniquely positioned to secure global leadership. Exports forecast for the Eleventh Plan period as estimated by NASSCOM McKinsey Report 2005 have been considered by the planners.

New Initiatives Sought

Debates on the information technology sector focus on technology development, entrepreneurship and innovation, and investment impetus. While building on the existing strengths base in the software sector, the economy has to muster its strength to meet shortage of trained human resource, bridging the digital divide and strengthening the IT hardware manufacturing base in the country for realising the goal of developing India into a regional hub for hardware manufacturing and exports. Our software industry needs to move up in the value chain from services to product development, and create Intellectual Property Rights (IPR).

Appropriate strategies encompassing fiscal and non-fiscal initiatives would need to be introduced in a coordinated manner to enable India to become a world leader in IT software and services, including ITES, and become a regional hub for IT and electronics hardware manufacturing. Taking advantage of the demographic dividend, we need to create a bank of highly trained manpower not only to meet the domestic requirement but also the rest of the world demand.

For achieving faster and inclusive growth many new initiatives are being taken. These include: (a) creation of integrated modern townships across the country for IT industries; (b) formulation of proactive IT-electronics hardware manufacturing policy; (c) development of trained manpower to meet the requirement of the industries on a continuous basis; and, promote R&D in few selected niche areas wherein we have the ability to become global leaders.

The demand for hardware is expected to grow at the rate of 30 per cent, as against 18 per cent at present. This would be fuelled by the aspirations of the younger generation and the large middle class in India with increasing disposable incomes. By the year 2010, the hardware market is expected to be of the order of US$ 85 billion. Keeping this in view, Electronics and IT Hardware Manufacturing has been identified as a thrust area. Major policy intervention on priority basis is required to promote the growth of the electronics/ IT hardware manufacturing industry so as to meet the growing demand.

Main Initiatives

Setting up of Integrated Modern Townships for Sunrise Industries, including IT and BPO, has been considered a priority area. IT industry lends itself for easy mobility and with the large number of educational institutions coming up across the country, there is a need to move the IT-ITES/BPO industries to tier-2 and tier-3 cities for promoting inclusive growth. In addition, it is also important to create "Information Technology Investment Regions" (ITIR) for setting up Integrated Modern Townships for Sunrise Industries including IT/ITES/ electronic hardware in the country.

Technology Development in Indian Languages has been identified as another area of priority. India is a multilingual country. There is, therefore, a need to provide user-friendly and cost-effective tools, applications and content that enable access to ICT infrastructure in Indian languages. The issues relating to linguistic data resource, content creation, language processing tools, and such technologies as optical character recognition, text-to-speech, speech recognition, cross-lingual information retrieval, and machine translation in multilingual environment are being addressed. To make available the fruits of IT development to the common man, fonts and software tools for some of the Indian languages like Hindi, Tamil, Telugu Assamese, Kannada, Malayalam, Marathi, Oriya, Punjabi and Urdu have been released in public domains. There is a need for developing similar software tools and fonts for other languages in the coming years.

A digital library of India is being created. Digital library offers many advantages over the traditional libraries. Having no physical boundaries and space constraints, the digital libraries are available round the clock with multiple accesses at multiple locations in a most cost effective way.

A National Knowledge Network can go a long way in bringing India to the forefront of education, science and technology, innovation, etc. The National Research and Education Networks (NRENs) are driving the pace of collaboration, innovation and discovery amongst scientists. Some of the major initiatives required in this direction include:

1. Creation of a suitable mechanism for setting up and operating a National Knowledge Network.
2. Connecting all major R&D establishments, central institutions, universities, colleges and libraries by using a dynamically configurable national multi-gigabit backbone network.
3. Empowering campuses through wireless network.
4. Having a Central Data Centre with 30 tera-byte storage, capable of expanding to peta-byte storage in future.
5. Creating a national educational portal which could host free educational content for e-learning

Virtual Skill Development Resource Network Linking through 50,000 Skill Development Centres. This multi-departmental scheme involving Department of Information Technology, Micro, Small and Medium Enterprises, Ministry of Rural Development, and Ministry of Textiles aims at creating 10 million skilled hands by setting up 50,000 Skill Development Centres, with skill development target of 200 person each.

School Connectivity

Education infrastructure needs to be strengthened and upgraded. In the first phase broadband access would be provided to every school. There are 1,08,000 government and government-aided schools in India. All these schools need to be put on the network progressively.

E-governance Investments

The following initiatives would be taken up for accelerating the national e-governance programme:

1. Encourage the central and state governments to procure e-governance services.
2. Fast replication of already successful e-governance programmes.
3. Make digital signatures mandatory for e-commerce, e-Government and e-banking initiatives.
4. Identify and develop "Killer Applications" – online auctions, e-voting, home banking, etc.
5. Speedy and effective implementation of various Mission Mode Projects (MMPs) under NeGP.
6. Promotion of technologies like xDSL, WiFI and WiMax for providing the last mile connectivity to places where copper wiring is not possible.
7. Technologies like BPL (Broadband on Power Lines) should also be explored.

R&D in the IT Sector

This support has helped in building infrastructure and competencies at a large number of academic and research institutions, and has produced the required manpower to take up R&D in the industry besides development of various products and packages. Some of the major thrust areas for R&D in the 11th plan include: ubiquitous computing, RFID, high performance computing, grid computing, high performance networking, bioinformatics, open source software, software engineering, web technologies, electronics–nanotechnology, photonics, micro-electronics, industrial electronics, automation electronics, embedded systems, and Electronics Material Development Programme.

Convergence of Bio-Info-Nano Technologies and Cognitive Science

The information and communication technology have already

converged leading to information and communication technology (ICT). Information technology combined with biotechnology has led to bioinformatics. Now, nanotechnology is knocking at our doors. It is the field of the future that will replace microelectronics and many other fields with tremendous application potential in the areas of medicine, electronics and material science, etc. Convergence of bio-nano-info technologies can lead to the development of nano robots. Likewise, a new revolution is also expected to be ushered in by the convergence of bio-info-nano technologies with the cognitive science in the coming years.

Key Constraints and Challenges

Some of the key constraints and challenges being faced by the IT and hardware manufacturing sector in the country are as follows:

1. *Small size/scale of operations:* The size and scale of operation of most manufacturing plants are very small compared to global market leaders. This leads to poor economies of scales for manufacturing as well as for sourcing. Lower capacities translate to higher per-unit overheads. Even though the cost of labour in India is low, it fails to offset the adverse impact of poor economies of scale.
2. *High rate of technological obsolescence:* Due to changes in technology, newer methods get introduced, calling for modern processes and equipment, which give a competitive advantage in terms of cost, speed and quality. Indian companies find it unviable to upgrade before the investments in earlier equipment are recovered.
3. *Unification of Manufacturing:* With rapid convergence of consumer electronics, IT and telecom and fast introduction of newer products in the market new vistas for the manufacture of accessories to support the new gadgets are emerging. Therefore, unification of product categories has to be attempted for manufacturing. Lack of credible and timely data on ICT usage (e-Stat) and its impact on the economy is a major constraint.

The Path Ahead

India's path ahead, as recommended by the Working Group and the Steering Committees is as follows:

1. Encourage state governments to initiate major citizen-centric mission projects under NeGP, preferably in PPP mode.
2. Promote electronics/ IT hardware manufacturing industry as it is one of the thrust areas of the Government of India.
3. A policy needs to be put in place to set up Hardware Manufacturing Clusters/ Parks in the private or public sector or public-private partnership and to co-locate the interdependent units in the same complex.
4. There is a need for a Policy for addressing the different issues related to the National Digital Library.
5. Operationalise the Unique ID Project to create a Core Data Base (CDB, using the most reliable pre-existing digitised database) which is then regularly updated and is easily accessible to, and used by all departments for identification of residents in the country for various purposes.
6. Initiate mission mode programmes and projects for developing quality human resource which is industry ready.
7. Initiate programmes for development of quality faculty.

3.2. Telecommunication

India's telecom market, estimated at $17.8 billion revenue in 2005; with a high growth rate of 36 per cent in 2004; and with 142 million subscribers (49 million fixed, and 93 million wireless) in March 2006; and 25 per cent annual average growth rate over a period of five years, is the world's fifth biggest market.

Status

During 2002-07, by 31 March 2007, the total telephone connections increased by 161.86 million achieving a teledensity of 18.31 per cent, exceeding the Tenth Plan target by 149 per cent. With the opening of the telecom sector to the private operators, their share in the number of subscribers has significantly increased.

Similarly, internet subscribers grew from 3.64 million in 2002-03 to 9.21 million in 2006-07; and the broadband subscribers count reached 2.28 million connections by 2006-07 from 1.8 lakh connections in 2004-05. One of the factors for such a low broadband subscriber base could be the pricing structure.

The number of telephones has increased to 206.83 million by 31 March 07, the number of mobile phone/ wireless subscribers increased to 166.05 million by 31.3.07, 90.15 per cent growth. The number of Internet subscribers grew at 23 per cent, while the broadband subscribers grew from a merger 0.18 million during 2004-05 to 2.28 million during the year 2006-07.

Mobile versus Fixed Telephones

The preference for wireless phones is clear from the rising share of wireless phones, which increased from 14.85 per cent to 80.28 per cent in 166.05 million telephones.

Trend in Teledensity

Whereas teledensity has been steadily increasing from 4.29 per cent, as on 31 March 02, to 18.31 per cent, as on 31.3.2007, a wide gap exists between urban teledensity (55.94%) and rural teledensity (2.83%). The rural telephony has not kept pace with the impressive growth in urban connectivity.

Rural Telephony

Apart from the 14.77 million fixed and Wireless in Local Loop (WLL) connections provided in the rural areas, 5,64,610 Village Public Telephones (VPTs) have also been provided. Thus, 90 per cent of the villages in India have been covered by the VPTs. In addition, more than two lakh Public Call Offices (PCOs) are also providing community access in the rural areas. The Mobile Gramin Sanchar Sewak Scheme (GSS) – a mobile Public Call Office (PCO) —service is also being provided at the doorstep of villagers. In order to provide Internet services, Sanchar Dhabas (Internet Kiosks) have been provided in more than 3,500 block headquarters out of the total 6,337 blocks in the country.

The telecom network in the rural areas also expanded during the Tenth Plan (2002-07). The number of phones in the rural area has increased from 9.01 million in March 2002 to 22.66 million by March 2007. The rural teledensity increased from 1.21 per cent in March 2002 to 2.83 per cent in March 2007. The bulk of the investment in rural telecom has been made by the public sector operator, viz., BSNL. The private operators had provided only 12,665 VPTs by the end of March 2006.

Planning Highlights

The Eleventh Plan focuses on the following as thrust areas:

1. Reaching a 600 million subscriber summit.
2. 200 million rural telephone connections by 2012 to attain rural teledensity of 25 per cent.
3. On demand telephone-connection at an affordable price.
4. To realise broadband policy 2004 target of 20 million broadband connections, and 40 million Internet connections by 2010.
5. 3G services in all cities/ towns with more than one lakh population.
6. To facilitate introduction of mobile TV.
7. Broadband connectivity to every secondary school, health centre, gram panchayat on demand in two years.
8. Making India a hub for telecom equipment manufacturing.

The planning debate focused on the following issues:

Network Expansion and Rural Telephony

1. One telephone for every three rural households by 2007, i.e., about 50 million rural connections.
2. One phone for every two rural households by 2010, i.e., about 101 million rural connections.
3. 200 million rural connections by 2012 (i.e. a rural teledensity of 25%).
4. For Rural telephony network expansion through: (i) market forces for viable areas; and (ii) Universal Services Obligation (USO) Fund for non-viable areas.
5. For providing public access in rural areas, the USO Fund will be provided for: (i) Village Public Telephones (VPTs); and, (ii) Rural Community Phones (RCPs).
6. For rural telephony the infrastructure will be shared at least amongst three service providers.
7. To support the development of general telecom infrastructure in rural areas, initially pilot projects would be undertaken for the same.

Broadband Coverage

Broadband coverage is important for both social well-being due to its role as a versatile medium of communication, and due to immense significance in the information and broadcasting economy of the country.

The planning stress on the equity in the development is on the following:

1. Broadband coverage for all secondary and higher secondary schools
2. Broadband coverage for all public health care centres.
3. Broadband coverage for all gram panchayats by 2010.
4. Linkage to be provided between block headquarters and nearest exchange for completing State Wide Area Networks (SWANs) connectivity.
5. Existing infrastructure of rural exchanges and Optical Fibre Cable (OFC) will be used.
6. Wireless technology will be deployed.

Manufacturing and R&D

1. Making India a hub for telecom manufacturing by facilitating more and more telecom specific Special Economic Zones (SEZs).
2. Providing a platform for export promotion of telephone equipment and services by setting up an Export Promotion Council.
3. Promoting research and development in key and emerging technologies appropriate for the country as well as in the area of telecom network security.

The Department of Telecommunication targets to take up the following programmes:

1. Making available adequate spectrum for both expansion of network and introduction of new value added services.
2. Setting up of Telecom Testing and Security Certification Centre (TETC).
3. Setting up of Centre for Communication Security Research and Monitoring.

4. Setting up of Next Generation Network (NGN) Laboratory.
5. Undersea-cabling between Mainland and Andaman & Nicobar (A&N) Islands.
6. Modernisation of Radio Spectrum Monitoring Capabilities.
7. Promoting induction of new technologies at Indian Telephone Industries (ITI).
8. Setting up of Telecom Export Promotion Forum/ Council for promotion of export of telecom services.

Constraints

1. Radio Frequency (RF) Spectrum is a limited resource, with competing and increasing demands, needing to have optimal and efficient use with greater sharing of this resource by all stake-holders. Effective RF Spectrum planning has to be carried out for short term, medium term and long term, taking into account the emerging new technologies.
2. Although a teledensity of 18.31 per cent has been achieved, there exists a wide gap between urban teledensity (55.94%) and rural teledensity (2.83%). Considering the fact that 70 per cent of the population lives in rural areas in India, the real challenge will be to connect rural India.
3. As voice-based connectivity (telephony) alone may not be the best economically viable option, therefore, the connectivity should predominantly be data based having killer applications to make it sustainable on which voice services can also be provided.
4. For an effective roll out the rural broadband connectivity would also need support through the Universal Services Obligation Fund (USOF).
5. To accelerate broadband connectivity, equipments need to be made available at an affordable price. In addition, local content in local languages need to be developed.
6. The transformation of traditional public telecommunications networks into Internet Protocol (IP)-based Next Generation Networks (NGN) will require significant technical, human as well as financial resources. Further activities relating to migration to Internet Protocol Version-

6 (IPv6) will have to be given priority, in order to spread Internet much faster.

7. Communication network needs to be adequately protected for which necessary network security-related initiatives need to be put in place.
8. The slow growth of telecom manufacturing sector is an area of major concern. The New Telecom Policy (NTP) 1999 sought to promote exports of telecom equipments and services. But till date the export of telecom equipment remains minimal. Most of the state-of-the-art telecom equipments, including mobile phones, are imported from abroad. There is, thus, an immense potential for indigenous manufacturing in India.

Policy Issues

The broad policy initiatives envisaged in key areas is as follows:

1. Re-framing of the Radio Frequency (RF) Spectrum keeping in view the needs of various sectors, keeping some spectrum space reserved for deploying new services, including for rural broadband, 3G, VoIP, etc. The spectrum allocation should follow international practices to enable India to enjoy economies of scale. Bringing in a regime of unified licensing could also be considered for most efficient utilisation of the allotted spectrum.
2. Promoting infrastructure-sharing by the service providers and incentivising such sharing for keeping overall costs down, especially to increase penetration telecom networks in rural areas.
3. Special attention needs to be paid to the most backward and remote areas, such as, the North-East, J&K, tribal belts and island authorities.
4. Suitable policy initiatives need for promoting telecom equipment manufacturing in the country, a coordinated approach to promote Public Private Partnerships (PPPs) for R&D activities in telecom equipment, formation of common product certification to International Standards and Testing Facility for Global Accreditation. Setting up of Mega FAB facility for the manufacture of Integrated

Circuits, Development of Hardware Manufacturing Cluster Parks (HMCPs), etc., also needs to be taken up to make India a telecom equipment manufacturing hub.

5. Adequate availability of international and national bandwidth at a low cost also needs to be ensured through appropriate technologies and policy interventions.

Special Issues in successful rollout of Rural Telephony and Broadband

Why does rural teledensity continue to be very low as compared to the present national average of 18.31 per cent. To answer this question what is being considered is this: (i) Proper Infrastructure for Access to Telecom Network; (ii) Suitable Access Devices; and (iii) Proper and adequate Content.

New Initiatives in the Telecommunication Sector

It is seen that broadband/bandwidth penetration has a multiplier effect on the economy. Experience in other countries has shown that broadband penetration has a positive correlation with the national income.

Despite a nearly 8,50,000 route kms of Optical Fibre Cable (OFC) infrastructure, the geographical availability of the bandwidth remains poor and expensive, and remains largely in the private hands. India has targeted 20 million broadband and 40 million internet users (connections) by 2010, which presupposes deeper PC penetration. This is more likely with government interventions like e-governance, rural connectivity, e-education with the consequential creation of bandwidth capacity, an increase in the penetration of PC, internet and broadband users.

Pricing Policy

Considering high price-sensitivity of Indian market, the acceptance of expensive telecommunications and bandwidth goods and services needs to be priced attractively.

Fiscal Policies

On the fiscal side the following steps need to be taken:

1. Encourage the availability of low-cost access devices.
2. Decrease duties on items used in broadband networks, and equalise duties on inputs for domestically manufactured goods and on finished imports.

3. Provide appropriate tax structure to enable growth, without having to forego significant revenue.
4. Coordination between PSUs should be established by encouraging BSNL coordinate with the consortium of PSUs – POWERTEL, GAILTEL and RAILTEL to identify clearly the additional villages that could be provided broadband connectivity by utilising the latter's network due to the nature of coverage provided by their network. Suitable financial incentives should be worked out by the USO administrator to facilitate this programme.

New Value Added Services

1. Internet Protocol Television (IPTV), by using point-to-point connection, uses multicasting techniques to give broadcasting effect of converging provisioning of voice, video and data – referred to as triple play – through a single medium. It can provide services of both cable TV service operators and telephony service operators. It is regarded widely as a the killer application for broadband, particularly in the rural areas.
2. Mobile TV, a hand-held device used for mobile TV reception, represents a four-way convergence referred to as quadruple-play. While the 3G for video transmission should bring in mobile TV in the normal course, Mobile TV promises great advantages in video reception at a frequency other than the one used for voice and data applications, as in FM radio on handsets.
3. Down-linking guidelines to be modified to permit broadcasters/content providers to provide their content to IPTV and Mobile TV service providers also. The technology enables the service providers to add their own content also on these platforms. Therefore, there will also be a need for regulatory mechanism to regulate the content on the IPTV and Mobile TV.

To continue to surge ahead, the Planning Commission stresses on the need for moving in the following direction:

1. World class infrastructure for supporting accelerated growth of all sectors, bridging the digital divide, an opti-

mum utilisation of spectrum, focus on policy recommendations for promotion of private sector investment, including FDI, and to take suitable initiatives for improving the performance of telecom equipment manufacturing sector.

2. Local content and applications are an important constituent for overall growth of Internet and broadband services. For achieving these goals the following major steps will have to be undertaken: (i) Facilitation for creation of multimedia and video content in the country; (ii) Devising proper incentive for development of regional and local language content; (iii) Thrust to the development of content and application for e-governance, e-education, e-health.
3. Effective promotion and diversified use of shared rural broadband infrastructure to provide new opportunities, augment income, promote overall development in the areas of tele-education, telemedicine and e-governance.
4. Online retail in a broadband environment to be promoted by coordinating the roles of such facilitators as Electricity Authorities, State IT Departments, Department of Local Self Governments, Panchayats, Department of Agriculture, Department of Health and Family Welfare, Department of Education.

3.3. Mass Communication

Mass communication gives impetus to the change and development in an economy and society. Ever since the beginning of the modern world, print media and radio have played a significant role in education, entertainment and information dissemination as the two media themselves underwent tremendous technological changes. In the meanwhile, there came television which further added new charms to media. As this print, the radio and television trinity of mass media ruled the world unopposed even while adding quality and colour, there came the fourth basic medium of mass communication: the Internet. The Internet since its birth, again underwent startling improvements now making possible interactive voice, data and image communication, both off-line as well as on online. Again when the world was busy adapting to the technological changes and skills for using these mass communication media for development and entertainment in the analogue mode, there came the digital avatar of them. The digital print, radio, television and internet have become the latest standards of development.

The world is working relentlessly to digitalise their mass-communication media. This, the experts believe, would go a long way to metamorphose their economies into digital economies, making them the fruits of heightened levels of economic activities possible by way of building value-addition and wealth-creation chains and on the existing economic, cultural and social structures.

Broadcasting Sector

India's broadcasting, All India Radio and Doordarshan, consists of 229 AIR analogue terrestrial radio (MW and SW) stations, 264 analogue private terrestrial stations and one private satellite radio, i.e., World Space. The television broadcasting set-up consists of 1,398 analogue terrestrial transmitters and four digital transmitters in public sector, 6000 MSO's, and 65,000 LCO's in private sector, three digital DTH satellite television operators in public and private sectors.

The News Service Division has among its various news-service networks now news-on-internet on its *www.newsonair.com*, which is a major initiative to bring the public radio broadcasting online for wider reach. The National Rural Health Mission (NHRM) has relied on AIR's broadcasting network through an 18-minute capsule for making necessary correction in the basic architectural correction in health care delivery system.

Significant digitalisation moves of AIR includes digitalisation of AIR Archive, releasing of Akashvani Sangeet, i.e. music, in digital formats, beginning of Data Radio Channel (DARC) system on existing FM radio network; six-channel Phone-in-Conference, interactive radio service.

Out of 210 million houses, by the 2001 census, television has reached 108 million, with cable and satellite in 68 million homes. The DTH subscription is around 5.6 million (DD DTH share 4.0 million, and private DTH 1.6 million). Similarly, the number of radio sets was 132 million. The total radio coverage by population has reached 99.13 per cent. There are, in all, 229 AIR and FM channels and 42 private FM stations.

Digitisation of Broadcasting Infrastructure

Digitalisation of complete AIR and Doordarshan involves digitisation of Up-link facilities for earth stations; down-link for stations from satellite; studio-to-transmitter links, procurement of equipments for Digital Satellite News Gathering facilities, and procurement of end-line equipments.

The digitisation programme of India for AIR and Doordarshan means replacement of all terrestrial transmitters by digital transmitters and digitisation of entire chain of facilities, including production facilities in studios, outside studios, and down-link and up-link facilities, studio to transmitters link, procurement of end line equipments. In view of this reality, the Eleventh Plan has allocated a substantial part of information and broadcasting sector outlays for digitalisation

The second set of related issue is creation of digital content compatible to high definition TV. This has gained maximum importance because it has become vital for the survival of public service broadcaster to achieve its threefold objective of entertainment, education and information in every single programme produced. During the Tenth Five Year Plan, the first time high quality content creation gathered serious attention to provide public service broadcaster a competitive edge vis-à-vis rapidly flourishing private broadcasting firms and rising broadcasting standards. In response to this, an alternative mechanism for creating rich content was devised by providing funds to institutions and individuals, known for professional excellence and high standards.

Press and Print Media

The Registrar of Newspapers for India established in 1956 under the Press Registration of Books Act, 1867, is a body responsible for annually reporting the status of press and print media. Indian press and print media are a huge mass consisting of 62,550 newspapers and periodicals. These include 6,800 dailies, 21,453 weeklies, and 8,227 fortnightlies, 18,545 monthlies, 4,340 quarterlies, and 584 annuals and around 2,601 publications of various other periodicity.

The language and culture panorama that the printmedia covers is so vast as to consist of 123 languages and dialects. The size of the Indian press and printmedia market can be gauged from the fact that principal languages listed in the Eighth Schedule of the Indian Constitution alone number 21, notwithstanding the giant presence of the English language. In terms of the number of newpapers and periodicals published, Hindi enjoys the first position with 24,017, and English second with 8,768.

Digitalisation is changing the press and printmedia scene in many ways. All major press and printmedia firms have gone on-line, and secondly their speed and networking have improved tremendously with digitalisation, out of which 128 companies have signed licences. The total number of Internet-users by March 2006 was estimated to be around 7.1 million.

Internet and Internet Infrastructure

It has become a new arena of economic activities never foreseen. By September 2006, 396 licences have been issued to companies for providing Internetservices. There are 31 companies engaged in setting and operating very small aperture terminals (VSAT) network via INSAT satellite system; and 11 commercial VSAT licences who provide services to Closed User Group Communication (CUG) to create shared Hub Infrastructure. Around 63,000 VSAT's and 260 earth stations are engaged in providing un-lining networks.

With multidisciplinary telecom solution providers like Telecommunication Consultants Limited engaged in concept to completion services to switching, transmission, rural communication, e-governance, e-education, telemedicine, etc., the Indian economy is forging ahead toward digital economy.

Vision and Strategy

Broadcasting

In the broadcasting sector the thrust is on the development of content in quality, coverage and convergence. The content development and variety should be so as to meet the need for digital broadcasting and high-definition television and radio broadcasting.

Content

The focus of content development should be on the following:

1. The public Service Broadcasting should focus on developmental programmes of the government and bringing in social awareness.
2. Reorganisation of Prasar Bharati.
3. With the re-emergence of radio as a medium of profound reach and impact, especially FM radio, AIR needs to forge partnerships with private FM players to expand and effectively utilise this medium.
4. Establish an International Channel through Public Private Partnership.
5. Facilitate emergence of India as an important source for high quality animation based content.

Expansion of transmission network, digitalisation and mobile media has to be achieved for going ahead with the work of high-definition TV and radio.

1. The DTH market has matured and the arrival of IPTV and mobile broadcasting is imminent and need to be nurtured.
2. With the convergence of technologies and availability of single gadgets with multiple applications, there are issues relating to policies, standardisation of infrastructure, practices and convergence which will need to be dealt with. One such issue is that of IPTV.
3. Digitisation of content and phasing out analogue broadcasting and creating an enabling environment for promotion of audio / video on demand.
4. Digital archiving of films acquired by National Films archives and produced by Films Division.
5. Introduction of HDTV broadcasting and removal of barriers for spread of DTT, DTH, IPTV and Mobile Broadcasting.
6. Articulation of an effective IPR protection regime for film, music and home-video.
7. FM coverage to be enhanced from 35 per cent to 45 per cent by using DRM+ compatible transmitters.
8. Border areas, rural areas and semi-urban areas to be accorded priority for FM coverage.
9. No further expansion of Doordarshan terrestrial network. However, emphasis should be on digitisation. VLPT's to go out of service on completion of their life. Border and

uncovered areas to be covered through technologies like DTH.

10. Private players' entry in the DD transmission network for providing mobile solutions and terrestrial transmission should be preferred through PPP route.

Miscellaneous Broadcasting Initiatives

The miscellaneous areas that need be focused on to enable the national development efforts achieve their targets are as follows:

1. Mobile media solutions on a fast track basis should be implemented to provide variety in entertainment platforms.
2. Digital transmission to be encouraged through Head-end in the Sky (HITS).
3. Evolving a Common Regulator for the Information, Communication & Entertainment (ICE) Sector is being considered. The earlier initiative to create a "Convergence Commission" with a "carriage bureau" and a "content bureau" needs to be revisited.
4. In the context of the general movement of technology in the direction of convergence, i.e. (a) convergence of network platforms (viz broadcast, satellite, cable, telecom) carrying similar kinds of services, and, (b) merging of consumer devices such as telephones, televisions, PCs, all capable of triple-play, is a pointer that increasingly all carriage networks and devices, will be able to carry all kinds of contents.
5. Early setting up of a Broadcast Regulator for resolution of legal and regulatory issues.
6. Following the formation of Information, Communication and Entertainment (ICE) Committee under the aegis of the PMO, in a subsequent meeting the PMO, a sub-group on digitalisation, another on band with related issues was formed, respectively named as Going Digital, and Sub-Group on Band Width. Headed by the then Member Secretary of Planning Commission, these two groups looked into various issues concerning these two areas of high priority. The main issues flagged and the recommendations made are discussed in the ensuing sections.

7. The milestones set by important nations are indicative of high priority. The milestones are: official date of launching digitalisation, start of closing down, and closing down. The United Kingdom, Sweden, Spain, Finland, Germany and Portugal have announced their milestones. Beginning with UK, which had launched digitals services in 1998, and Sweden in 1999, and by 2003, all these countries had launched digital services. By 2008, all these countries were to start closing down. Sweden, Finland and Germany were to close down by 2008. What is noticeable in these cases is that a longer time was taken to begin closing down after launching of digitalisation, which was 10 years in UK, six years in Sweden, eight years in Spain. The time taken for the next milestone, close down, was four years in UK, two years in Sweden, and two years in Spain. It appears that depending on the size of infrastructure and resource availability time taken in beginning to close down can be longer on account of national policy, but the complete shift to digital system depends on the comfort level required by the consumers to gear up to buy new receivers, the ability to pay, and the government's compulsion to shorten the switching over period in view of high costs of simulcasting during this period.
8. In view of the enormity of India's public service broadcaster's size, the overall limitations, the global digitalisation scene, the Going Digital Sub-Group identified a migration-path for India which is as follows:
   i) Testing publication and adoption of technical standards for digital terrestrial transmission.
   ii) Publication and adoption of technical standards for digital cable television.
   iii) Prasar Bharati's rollout plan for transmission conversion, i.e., from analogue terrestrial to digital terrestrial transmission for AIR and Doordarshan.
   iv) Introduction of addressability and conditional access system in cable and satellite TV environment.
   v) Road map and commencement of indigenous production of STB's containing (a) digital analogue conversion for delivery of digital signal, at subscribers'

end; and, (b) conditional access and addressability features.

vi) Publication, and adoption of national digital television standards for manufacture of digital receivers.

vii) Commencement of indigenous production of digital receivers.

viii) Commencement of digital terrestrial broadcast in selected cities by Prasar Bharati in the following sequence:
Step I : Delhi by 2010
Step II : All mega cities by 2011
Step III: All tier II and Tier III cities by 2012
Step IV: All other cities by 2013.

ix) Commencement of HDTV broadcast with Commonwealth Games in 2010 by Prasar Bharati.

x) Commencement of digital signal delivery at subscribers' end in cable and satellite homes.

xi) Switching off analogue to both terrestrial and C&S (cable and satellite) homes by 2015.

9. Equally important were non-broadcasting digitalisation issues: regulatory and legal ones. The issue is related to the emerging technological convergence, and the question whether a common regulator or separate regulating bureau system would suit.

3.4. Path Ahead

The Path Ahead consists in transforming the information, broadcasting as well as the media and entertainment sector, into a modern, efficient and responsive entity. To achieve this objective, in addition to putting in place necessary policy interventions and barriers to investment in the entertainment and media industry, the country needs effectively to address the following issues:

1. Lack of uniformity in media policy for foreign investment (FDI) limits in different sectors – DTH (49%), Cable (49%) and Content (26%) for news on television and print and 100 per cent for non-news in TV & Print 20 per cent in radio and 100 per cent in film industry. This necessitates

harmonisation, and rationalisation of tax-treatment of foreign companies.

2. While policy enunciation imposes an obligation to observe cross-media ownership rules on media companies, these rules have not been formalised so far. The print and electronic media integration could result in the emergence of media behemoths acquiring a mind-share disproportionate to what is permissible in a competitive market environment. Some boundary limits need to be laid down, and this issue needs to be revisited for the sake of long-term health of the industry.

3 Incentivising the consumer and equipment manufacturers for successful roll out of Conditional Access System (CAS) and DTH across the country and timelines need to be fixed so that all the stakeholders could put their acts together.

4 Digitisation of satellite transmission, production centres/ studios, and terrestrial transmission needs to be undertaken in mission mode along with introduction of HDTV, IPTV, mobile TV and other value added services. For the broadcasting sector "Going Digital" and "Farming out Excess Bandwidth" need to be taken up expediently to ensure switching over to digital trans-mission by 2015 and optimal use of scarce bandwidth.

Virtual Skill Development Resource Networking

A massive virtual skill development resource networking for training people at doorsteps targeting at 10 million people during the Eleventh Plan was conceived. Designed to execute through 50,000 Skill Development Centres, this scheme would be implemented with the involvement of Department of Information Technology, Micro, Small and Medium Enterprises, and Ministry of Textiles. The institutional networks rope in for carrying out this skill development project are: 1 lakh Common Service Centres (CSC's) set up by Ministry of Telecom and IT; 10,800 IT-supported secondary schools; 1,47,000 rural post offices or panchayats. The execution strategy consists of 8-12 weeks programme on the basis of training material developed by participating industries, such as NASSCOM, mentor groups formed out of industry participants, and provision of toolkits provided by industry associations or state governments and marketing the skills in employment melas.

E-Governance Initiatives

The major e-governance initiatives are as follows:

Unique Identifiers UID for Indian residents, for corporate business entities, and smart cards are three areas of priority at present. These identifiers would add to a core-data base for different proposes.

Service Delivery Infrastructure

To provide support to the back end computerisation for enabling any time any where service delivery, in addition to the MISSION MODE PROJECTS (MMP's), a service delivery infrastructure is required to be created. In the Eleventh Plan, several projects serving this need were out in place. These include STATE WIDE AREA NETWORK (SWANS), Common Service Centres (CSCS), connectivity for the last mile project, leveraging BSNL rural exchanges, wireless connectivity from BSNL, last mile connectivity through UNIVERSAL SERVICE OBLIGATION FUND ('SOF) and State Data Centres.

SWANS is targeted at establishing an intra-government network in 29 states and six UT's; CSCS is aimed at establishing 100,000 broadband internet enabled kiosks in rural areas and similarly 100,000 in semi-urban areas; the last mile connectivity scheme is for making available connectivity infrastructure through BSNL and SOF.

ICT for Better Planning, Implementation, and Monitoring

ICT has found its application in formulation of better planning by ensuring better information inputs. Use of ID can be made in checking inflated schemes by eliminating inflated quantities and rates, bogs registration, registration of the dead, fraudulent requisitions for funds, inflated muster and fraudulent wages.

Secondly, in the use of ICT in major flagship programmes of the Eleventh Plan the government made it compulsory for all the line departments to make use of e-governance in conception, formulation, implementation and monitoring of flagship projects like NeGP, Bharat Nirman, PMGSY and NREGA.

The e-Health Scheme

The idea of forming a national health care grid, by involving health care providers, trainers, beneficiaries, and the civil society, had led to a successful operation of many pilot projects by private concerns, NGO's and medical institutions. From this emerged the initiative of Health Management Information System, and the possibility of telemedicine. With an appreciable beginning of telemedicine during the Tenth Plan, when such schemes as Jan Swasthya Sahyog (JSS) were experimented with, the Eleventh Plan included many important areas. These components of e-health included the following:

1. Training, education and capacity building for e-health.
2. Monitoring by e-enabled HMIS to ensure timely flow of data, and collation to be used at various levels.
3. GIS for resource mapping of health facilities, laboratories, training centres, man power, and other inputs for better planning of services.
4. Providing service delivery and other e-enabled activities, like disease surveillance, tele-consultations, health helpline, district hospital referral net, and e-enabled mobile medical units.

Made possible with participation of ISRO, DIT, Government of India, NEC Telemedicine programme for North-East; State governments, NGO's, various projects have been formed for the 11th Plan. These projects include NE Project, J&K Project, Armed Forces Medical Services Project, and many private projects, such as Asia Heart Foundation South India Project, Apollo Hospitals Project, etc.

Under the 11th Plan a provision of Rs.183.00 crore was kept for e-health programme.

Eleventh Plan Investment

Eleventh Plan Investment on Information, Communication and Telecommunication, and IT-enabled schemes indicate the importance of IT sector in the country's visions. Information, Communication and Telecommunication departments together drew an allocation of Rs. 1,06,069.00 crore out of the total eleventh Plan outlay of Rs.21,56,571 crore. The investments under various programmes as listed below those under the three departments specifically show the national effort for abridging the digital divide gaps in the developments of various regions and communities.

What one must understand is that every developmental effort in the areas of telecommunication, information technology, and information and broadcasting, is a step toward digital world economy. Department of Telecommunication's all 10 schemes, including wireless monitoring and planning, C-DOT, telecom engineering, under-sea cabling, technical assistance in telecom, an optical fibre network for defence, have massive digitalisation impact on the economy. Similarly, The Department of Information Technology's schemes, such as research and development, infrastructure development, human development and others have digital economy-enabling components. Finally, the Information and Broadcasting Ministry has information, film and broadcasting sector-related schemes with heavy digital economy enabling components. The ministry has focused on digitalisation of the entire process of information and communication.

Table 3.1: Eleventh Plan Investment on ICT and IT-based Development Activities

(Figures in Rs. crores)

Department/Activities	*Tenth Plan*		*11th Plan*
	Outlay	*Expenditure*	*Outlay*
Telecommunication	76,338.00	7,7244.00	89,582.00
Information Technology	5,492.00	2,674.00	11,048.00
Information & Broadcasting	5,130.00	2,802.00	5,439.00
Total	91,229.00	856,720.00	106,069.00
*School Education and			
Literacy – ICT in Schools			6,000.00
*IT for masses			150.00
*IT Infrastructure			7,087.00
*IT in Health			
e-Health			183.00

Note: Starred (*) entries indicate single activity investments in different Departments/Ministries, and they may or may not be additional vis-à-vis the ICT sector investment indicated in the table.

But the components that are singly targeted at digital economy development essence are Rs.6000 crore scheme of School Education and Literacy which has an ICT-in-school programme scheme. Similarly, IT for masses, IT Infrastructure, and IT in Health are key digital economy promotion activities with emphasis on covering the spatial and social disadvantaged.

4

National Digital Agenda: An Analysis of the Issues

For analysing India's digitisation agenda one has to look into a long list of domestic and global issues. This includes issues related to the new world economy of information and technology; the digital agenda of Government of India, as it appears from such documents as the Eleventh Five Year Plan, Vision 2020, important policy papers, in response to the global digital economy realities; India's own spectacular growth in information, communication and telecommunication. All these factors suggest that India is on the verge of experiencing her great developmental leap at this opportune moment of world development spurt.

India is facing twofold challenges: ensuring effective implementation of the agenda set before the nation; and watching out for irreversible socio-economic and environmental effects, especially those which increase vulnerability of socio-economically and spatially marginalised segments of population. Watching out for socio-economic and environmental side-effects on the marginalised and the disadvantaged is important because of India's recent development experience. Even as benign a development effort as irrigating vast expanses of farm land by big-dam projects had ruined millions of people from socio-economically prone segments of the society; and deprived the country of its large forests and fertile farm lands, making climatic disasters imminent. Neither the tens of millions of the displaced tribals and other remote river valley villagers could ever be rehabilitated and resettled, nor could we create even a single example of compensatory forests that can pass off as a forest. A classic case of irreversible side-effects.

In the context of digitalisation, technological convergence and the new world economy, the challenge is that of ensuring a development strategy that enables everyone to taste the fruits of *I way*. The new economy realities, as well as the present national agenda to make information, communication and telecommunication development more inclusive, it becomes imperative to ensure a socio-economically and regionally balanced development of the country.

This primarily necessitates evolving a holistic strategy which can ensure at every stage of economy, business, governance, civil society and polity, that the interest of the disadvantaged is not glossed over in the global race of corporate excellence, high economic growth, and the aggressive interest group tug of war.

4.1. Digitalisation and Convergence issues

Establishing proper IT-infrastructure and software capabilities, especially optical fibre networks, fibre to home networks; and a suitable identification and certification infrastructure by evolving public key infrastructure (PKI) are the major concerns of the developed and developing countries in digital development.

4.2. Internet Pricing

The connectivity issue of pricing with three layered routers and software is another important area of concern. These are Internet service providers (ISP); the end users; and, the major Internet backbone providers (IBPs). Given that the IBP's are world class telecommunication conglomerates and the final receivers, i.e., end-users, are identified, the problem lies in the uncertainty of the intermediary routes through which messages travel. Connectivity pricing which are dictated by IBP's wholesale prices are required to be effectively monitored and controlled, which brings in the issues of an effective regulatory system.

The economics of internet pricing is based on, first, cost of: (a) connecting to network, (b) additional network capacity, (c) social cost of congestion. And, the second determinant is pricing mechanism, which can be: (a) flat rate, (b) usage sensitive rate, including a connectivity bill based on per bit charge for any message received, transaction based price depending on the nature of the transaction. Government has to play a regulatory role in managing Internet pricing. Making Internet pricing effective would make possible wider use of this medium for all developmental and personality enrichment.

Internet-Market Structure and Regulation

Regulation is a major concern due mainly to internet market structure. There are mainly two market forms working: the one-way model, and the two-way model. In the one-way model there is a dominant service provider who provides service access to end-users, but without similar access from the other end, and the ISP provider provides transit services through IBP's. This market structure tends to be exploitative, unless regulated. The second model is the one in which there is no dominant firm, and two-way access is possible. This is more competitive and healthy. To ensure competitive pricing and fair competition among the service providers price-capping and unbundling mechanisms or policies are used. This unbundling basically means taking away the dominant service providers' hold on his service components, and fixing a competitive price.

Standards

Standards in cell phones, digital TV, coding and decoding, and business models have become competitive and intellectual property rights (IPRs) issues are involved. Differentiating between market induced *de facto* standards and mandatory standards is getting more difficult. This is another area of policy concern.

Multi-faceted gaps

Digital divide, as a multi-faceted problem, exists within the developed world, between the developed and the developing world; and between the rich and the poor within a developing country owing to uneven spread of conditional capabilities.

4.3. Acceptance of Digital TV

Internet conflict between cable TV, satellite TV, broadcasting stations, computer industry are casting uncertainties in television's future. The cost-reducing tendency of technology is another source of transformation and uncertainty of digital TV's future. The consumers' tendency to remain satisfied with analogue technology tends to keep the pace of change slow, and to that extent the complete shift to digital technology becomes slow.

4.4. Content

India's television broadcasting, in spite of fast move towards digitalisation, and gearing up to develop high-definition television infrastructure in a definite way is likely to face an acute shortage of quality content in compatible format. The major reason for this situation is that until very recent everything that was being produced was in analogue, and whatever being generated at present is a minuscule fraction of what is in demand. The historical reason for not having enough high quality content was the public service broadcaster's inability to produce enough in-house, and limited success of outsourcing content creation when it alone was large body responsible for it. The immediate cause for this acute shortage is a sudden spurt in broadcasting in so many regional languages without adequate fresh-content creation. The regional language channels being small payers with scanty resources have little resources at hand, while the content production industry is undeveloped. As a result of this, the vernacular channels, even including Hindi, could be seen starving of fresh content of high quality. Rather one can see an apparent disinterest in investing on high quality programme production.

But as far as the Public Service Broadcast is concerned, one major way of ensuring high quality, revenue generating programmes could be cost-effective and professional utilisation of its budgetary resources through a network of non-governmental organisation, or a trust of existing eminent media people engaged in these activities. Set up in the line of a trust, such as Public Service Broadcast, these agencies can be used as an autonomous body entered into an MoU with the public service broadcaster for producing innovative content in need, and as requisitioned by the public service broadcaster. Beginning with a partnership at the central government level, a similar MoU can be entered into a state level for meeting the regional broadcasting needs.

The simple economic strength of this arrangement lies in the fact that with the same or a fraction of the budgetary resources, the broadcaster would be able to produce programmes in time, with professional excellence that attracts larger viewing or listening audience, and raises commercial value (advertisement worth) of the programmes while serving the socio-economic goals of entertaining, informing and educating people.

4.5. Emerging Social Issues

Digital technology and convergence in internet, broadcasting, entertainment, publishing are causing distortions in an individual's personal and social life. As if the TV's social interaction reducing impact was not enough, now each individual member of a family remains glued to the keyboard, spends long times online than with the family members. Moreover, Internet takes one away from the real world, and turns into virtual world recluse. A child is so busy playing CS (Counter Strike), a violent interactive online game on the LAN (local area network) available in broadband service, that he wakes up till late night until intervened. His appetite for story books, and inclination to participate in various family social occasion in the family and in the neighbourhood has declined.

The popularity and vast use of Internet-based input devices are making an impact on language and all that is related to the system of symbolism that makes language and communication. The Internet natives, those born in the Internet age, have quietly degenerated their language of communication in diminutives and abbreviations and effortless expressions. The kids are getting into a language that is dirty and distorted.

A new type of crimes originating from the Internet world, such as leakage of personal information, stealing of credit card numbers, hacking and computer virus attacks, has begun to invade the society.

The very nature of IT-based business and infrastructure has serious impact on relocating personnel in multinational firms, and indirectly replacing old technical hands by new ones, and causing changes in the pattern of employment by bringing in workers with skills rather than with production profile.

Policy Issues

The experiences of other countries, like that of Thailand, highlight the policy a country has to deal with. First, liberalisation of telecom market is the way to overcome state monopoly of telecom infrastructure monopoly, and to benefit customers, existing and new operators, employees, and domestic and foreign investors. Second, the Human Resource Development (HRD) sphere face IT talent brain-drain from low-paid industry to high-paid industry, from less IT advanced to high IT advanced countries, from traditional to new sectors, from the small and medium scales to large scale firms.

India has already Telecom Regulatory Authority of India (TRAI) as its regulatory arm, without finally resolving the issue whether in view of the experience so far it should go for the separate regulatory bureau solution to ensure effective tackling of the regulatory problems in various spheres of information and communication technology. The bandwidth segment of the problem is lying unattended, even though some efforts are going in this direction. The teething problem here too lies in the reality that those who have excess bandwidth in their possession see it as their future wealth, and value the opportunity cost they had borne in keeping them for this purpose. What needs to be done is to obtain excess bandwidth available with various organisations on the basis of compensation package evolved to benefit the economy as a whole while not making the bandwidth owners not worse off.

As regards the HRD brain-drain issue, there appears to be no effective and plausible solutions. The fact that in a market economy every factor of production is free to receive the highest returns leaves no scope for any effective ways out. But some standards even within this economic freedom framework can be evolved for transparency and effectiveness.

4.6. Regional Cooperation and Government

For an IT amenable human resource development, a government may have to resort to regional cooperation for enabling itself to perform many roles sought in the wake of socio-economic pressures. An assistance package can be sought from an IT-experienced country for solving problems. The assistance can be focused on: (a) raising awareness of IT opportunities and contributing intellectually to policy and institutional building; (b) providing technical assistance for training people in IT skills and management; (c) building IT-infrastructure and providing assistance for networked establishment; and, (d) promoting IT-based developmental programmes such distance development training, distance education, training, healthcare and governance.

Even though India has a grand plan for ensuring every aspect of digitalisation and technological convergence and simulating digital economy, yet what is doubtful is its absorption capacity, the economic metabolism, which needs enormous resources even when funds are available. It is here that regional cooperation programmes for raising awareness for IT-opportunities, capacity building, trainings, managerial skills, and for ensuring IT-infrastructure and networked establish-ment are important.

4.7. World Bank and UN Concerns for Digital Divide

The World Bank stresses on investment on establishment of

telecentres, while UN agencies have focused on the creation of electronic community centres as platform for access and connectivity in rural areas, and centres for capacity building, skill enhancement, training, communications and content development. SME's are encouraged to use these facilities and develop websites, digital management, and e-commerce.

5

Is National Capital Region IT Conducive?

5.1. A Case Study

Why Delhi?

Why was Delhi chosen for the case study? One major reason was Delhi's suitability as a metropolitan with ideal clusters of population with urban, suburban and rural areas in close vicinity. Accessibility to sample population clusters easily, availability of representative and balanced sample families for study were other factors favouring Delhi as the ideal case study. Statistically speaking, Delhi has ideal conditions for discerning the effect of each determinant on the level of conduciveness due to comparable conditions in other respects. For example, IT-conduciveness can be ascribed to literacy when other conditions more or less remain comparable due to locational proximity between urban Delhi and suburban Delhi, and between urban Delhi and rural Delhi. To understand this point, consider as to what would be the results if the samples were drawn from typical urban and typical rural villages located hundreds of miles apart.

The sampling method used had the following features:

1. Pre-survey visits were made to sample areas identified on such consideration as spatial spread in terms of urban, suburban and rural areas. The idea behind this three-level sampling in Delhi was to know the differences in the spread of digital economy's fruits across spatial spread of Delhi even while focusing on the social strata. It was felt that comparing a typical metro sample with a far-flung sample population might not show any meaningful result. Moreover, in view of better reach of IT and ICT, and

broadcasting infostructure and skills in advanced areas of Delhi, the sample was likely to be more balanced. Comparing an advanced and typical metro population cluster with its suburban population and then with its adjacent rural population would be more ideal. This would yield a sample that can reveal the typical effects of spatial, social and economic prosperity factors. Therefore, sample families were drawn from South Delhi's Defence Colony, Laxmibai Nagar, and Pillengi village; as well as from sub-urban cluster of Punjabi Basti, and from Mukund Pur village in Delhi.

2. The composition of the sample was determined following the multi-stage stratified sampling design. According to this method, sample households were drawn from all the three locations of Delhi considering their representativeness from all angles. This required picking up 18 sample families from South Delhi, keeping in view geographic spread between rural and urban areas; social strata of SC and OBCs. Similarly, 28 families were selected in the suburban Delhi's Punjabi Basti. Finally 56 families were drawn from Mukund Pur village. The number of the General, the SC and the OBC categories in the total sample was roughly in proportion to their ratio in the total local pattern. Finally, within each social and spatial sample population high, middle and low income families were selected for maintaining an economic strata representativeness in the total sample population.
3. The survey was carried out to understand the relationship between socio-economic and geographical factors, and the spread of IT, ITES, and skills and facilities conducive to enjoying benefits of ICT as a whole in the emerging digital economy. The survey has a sample size of 100 families, and was conducted through a direct questionnaire.

Questionnaire Design

A questionnaire with three parts was designed. The first part was designed to capture relevant data on the family's social strata, literacy, occupation, income and skills; the second part focused on computing and communication information; and the third part was about IT and ICT familiarity.

The data gathered by field survey was then organised and computed and tabulated to get information on the following:

1. Computing facilities vis-à-vis social status income and life-style.
2. Communication facilities vis-à-vis lifestyle, income and surroundings and occupation.
3. Entertainment, publication and information use pattern.
4. ICT employment pattern in relation to social strata, education, skills and geographical location.
5. Place of computer and internet familiarity in overall priority.
6. IT future in people's perception.
7. What needs to be done for widespreading IT: people's suggestions.
8. What ails the present cable TV multi-casting?

Objectives of the Survey

This case study was made to understand the socio-economic and socio-geographical inequalities that exist in the distribution of government and private infostructure. Knowing this aspect is important in the context of the country's much-talked-about transformation into digital convergence technology age and digital economy, which means a massive upsurge of economic activities in information technology, IT enabled-services, telecommunication, broadcasting, entertainment, data-processing, and BPO's and KPO's.

The 'Digital Delhi' is going to happen before or around the Commonwealth Games 2010. One pertinent question that rises in the mind of the thinking lot is how well-disposed is this metro-capital-city population for enjoying this superlative status in a more democratic way. Is it anywhere near digital-democracy, the I-Way of equality in terms of orientation to digital life, employment, income, and revolution in economic opportunities in IT and IT-enabled services.

Knowing well that the much hyped technology boons and the mushrooming of IT-enabled services are limited to the lucky few who have suitable schooling background, specific professional qualifications and enjoy money-power, the moot question is to ascertain as to how many people in general and those in the disadvantaged socio-economic and spatial strata, in particular, are experiencing any change on account of this development, and, how well-equipped they are to avail the advantages of the paradigm-shift in their existential concerns in the digital economy and society.

Since the three C's encompass the entire gamut of activities, structures, skills and products, it is necessary to know the status of each sample family and cluster with regard to them. Computing facilities, such as PC and software, and other gadgets as mobile, camera, etc., give the most substantial data about meeting the basic condition for availing IT and IT-enabled services. Second, the communication facilities, i.e., telephony, satellite and wireless, provide for the basic infostructure required for availing the present analogue cable services multi-casting services, and the fully digital future services. The content composition, audio-video entertainment, information, education, spiritual or literary, or cultural productions available in various mediums, gives an idea about the kind of content consumption that goes in the Indian market.

Similarly, the study also endeavoured to throw light on where lies the infostructure in the modern lifestyle priorities of the urban, suburban and rural folks. Instead of asking the interviewee to indicate their priorities, the data regarding type of houses, TV, car, mobike, mobile was collected.

The Sample Population

In aggregate, the surveyed sample population had 100 families with a population size of 570. This had a total general category population of 158 in 40 families, (See Annexure 1). The SC sample population size had 151 in 26 families. The OBC category had a population of 205 in 36 families. In South Delhi's typical urban sample all three categories are dominated by higher income strata; in suburban Delhi's Punjabi Basti, the sample could catch very few high income strata, and is dominated by lower income and some middle income families. But the scene in typical rural set-up of Mukund Pur village is dominated by lower income and middle income families. In consideration of the local economic conditions and pre-survey discussions, the high income middle income, and lower income strata were defined as with a combined annual income of above Rs.2 lakh rupees; between Rs. 1 lakh and Rs.2 lakhs; and those with income below Rs.1.00 lakh. What is apparent from this survey is that except for the South Delhi urban population sample, all other segments of sample population is surviving at or below Rs. 1 lakh annual income. Please see Annexure 4.

Urban Population

The spatial break-up of urban, suburban and rural sample was: 17 families from South Delhi's general, SC and OBC families, consisting of 10 general category families, 2 SC families, and 5 OBC families. In each group high, middle and low income strata were sampled. The terms used is GCH, GCM, GCL, standing for general category high income, middle income, and low income families. Similarly, for the SC families and OBC families, the terms denoting their social and income groups are SCH, SCM, SCL; and OBCH, OBCM, and OBCL. The category-wise sample population is: general category 46, SC 8, OBC 83. Please see Annexure 1.

Suburban Population

The suburban Punjabi Basti sample population has a sample household numbering 28 families, with a category-wise break-up of 12 general category, 10 SC and 6 OBC families. The respective population was 56, 63 and 34. This population size is in tune with the local population composition.

Rural Population

Mukund Pur is a typical plains village with proximity to a major city, and still living eons away from the real manifestation of urban standards in its life. This village with around one lakh population has around 40:60 ratio in its general category to others' population. The sample size had a general category component of 18 families with a population of 112, SC segment of 14 families with population of 80, and finally 23 OBC families with a population of 142.

Ten-Point IT-conduciveness Scale

Let us first see the socio-economic and the socio-geographic spread of infostructure and attainments that together determine the status of the sample population. To simplify, and make the result more striking, all the elements of computing and communication facilities, and those of content were arranged in seven columns of information vis-à-vis each family in various socio-economic and spatial profile. While determining their weight in the scale, each of the attribute was assigned weights between 1 and 2. The scale was, however, so arranged as to bring the most commonly found infostructure and attainment attributes at the top, and the others below them. Thus, the ten-point scale has cable or satellite TV on the top; with cable, mobile, telephony, computer, email or online transactions, and ownership of personal computer placed subsequently. Attributes related to familiarity to computer as pattern of use and ownership of computer are assigned 2 points, and others 1 point each.

The status of the sample families has been stated in terms of one figure, ranging between one and ten. Please, see Table 1 and details given in Annexure 2.

5.2. Findings

Cable and Satellite TV Houses

Only 71 of the total population of 101 families surveyed were connected with cable or satellite TV, and the number of people using satellite connection is nominal. The connectivity variation across rural and urban social set-up is sharper than that in the social strata, which indicates the entertainment and information necessity feature of the communication media. (See Table 1, and Annexure 2.)

The urban families have cent-per-cent cable, broadband, Internet and satellite connections in its high income general category families, i.e., all the 10 general category families had cable or satellite connectivity. Similarly all the SC and the OBC families had this connection.

The suburban segment of urban Delhi, as evident from the Punjabi Basti case, has cable or satellite connection in 89 per cent houses. Social category-wise distribution shows that all the general category families had cable or satellite TV connections, while the SC and the OBC families had near 100 per cent connections.

The total urban area scene of cable and satellite TV connection indicates that out of 45 families studied, only 40 families have cable or satellite TV connections, which indicates a low 89 per cent connectivity, with the SC and the OBC families are yet to reach complete connectivity.

The rural connectivity scenario is different. Out of 56 families studied only 31 had cable or satellite TV connections, indicating only 55 per cent coverage. The social strata-wise scenario reveals that 61 per cent of general category houses, and 71 per cent of SC houses, and 92 per cent of OBC houses had connectivity. The reason for lower connectivity in general category houses is that the entire sample families, except one, fell in the low income bracket. On the other hand, among the SC and OBC sample population there are a considerable number of middle income groups.

Mobile and Telephony

In the total sample population of 570, in 100 families, number of families with mobiles is 75, and those with telephone connection are 71. This indicates that a predominant number of families have at least one mobile and a telephone connection. The distribution patterns of mobile and telephony connection was studied in terms of spatial spread and socio-economic strata. The number of families having both mobile and telephone connection in the general category is 10, which means cent-per-cent availability of these two connectivity in the urban Delhi. As compared to the general category sample families, 50 per cent scheduled caste families have at least one mobile, 50 per cent have telephones. As far as the OBC segment of urban Delhi is concerned more families have telephony connection than mobile phones. Out of five OBC families only three has mobile, while five have telephones connections.

The mobile and telephony connection scenario becomes different as one moves to the suburban segment of Delhi's urban region. In the 28 family sample size, with 153 population, 22 families have mobiles connections, and 25 families enjoy telephony, indicating that 89 per cent houses have at least one mobile phone and 79 per cent houses had telephones. This means close to complete coverage. In the social strata-wise distribution, the survey reveals that the general category families, numbering 18, have mobile connection in 10 families, with telephone connections in 12 families. This pattern of dispersion indicates the influence of literacy percentage, age composition, and occupation in this category. Similarly, among the SC segment of the sample population, numbering 10 families, the number of families with mobile connection is seven, and that with telephones is eight. In the case of OBC segment, with five families, the number of families with mobile connection is three, while telephone connection is 100 per cent.

In the income group-wise distribution of mobile and telephone connection among these suburban families, it is found that the coverage of mobile and telephone connectivity is incomplete only in the middle and lower income groups of general category, the SC and the OBC.

In the same way, the mobile and telephone connectivity on the aggregate level, i.e., including both urban and suburban sample clusters of South Delhi and Punjabi Basti, indicates that out of the total sample family of 46 the number of families having mobile connection is 37, and that with telephones is 40, indicating percentage of houses with mobiles and telephone as 61 per cent, and 87 per cent respectively. Availability of these two key connectivity is important.

Let us now see the mobile and telephone connection status in the typical rural area of Delhi. In the sample family size of 56 households, the number of families having mobile connections and telephones are 38 and 31, respectively. This means only 68 per cent families had mobile connections; and only 55 per cent families had telephones connections in rural Delhi.

The social strata wisespread of these two important connectivities indicates that out of 18 families in the general category only seven (39%) families have mobile connections while 11 (61%) have telephones. On the other hand, among 14 SC families the number of the ones with mobile connection and telephones is 10 each. As regards the OBC families, out of the sample of 23 families have mobile connections and 23 telephones. The variation in the connectivity distribution among the three categories in terms of lower connections in the general category can be explained by the fact that the general category sample families happen to be in the lower income strata.

Acquaintance with Computer and Internet

Regarding acquaintance with computer and internet, the focus was on ascertaining the level of familiarity with the ability to use computer and Internet facilities. The survey collected data on use of computers, e-mails and availability of computers in the sample families. Please see Annexure 3. The data thrown up by the study indicates that in the total population, 113 persons know the use of computers and Internet, indicating that 20 per cent of the population are familiar with computers and also use Internet.

In the urban population of 83, about 40 persons, i.e., more than 50%, are familiar with computers and also use e-mails. As regards availability of computers, almost every family has a computer. The status of social strata-wise familiarity with computers and Internet use indicates that among the general category people the number of persons familiar with computers and Internet is 20 each, which means more than 20%. The availability of personal computer is seven in this group, which indicates 70 per cent. But familiarity with computers and Internet is far lower among the SC and the OBC segment of the sample area. Only 50 per cent of the sample SC families have familiarity with computers and internet, and availability of computer is up to 50 per cent. The position in the OBC segment is far worse. In a population of 29 only 12 persons have acquaintance with computers and also know use of Internet. As regards availability of computers, all the five sample families in the OBC category have computers.

Among the suburban sample population of 153 only 52 persons, i.e., 34 per cent, were found to be familiar with computers and 41, i.e., 27 per cent, use internet also. The availability of computer is limited to only nine, i.e., 3.8 per cent, families out of 28 families that have been studied. Interestingly, among these suburban families there were people with experience of using Internet in daily transaction. The percentage share of people using computers and Internet in the suburban population segment is far lower than those in the urban areas.

The combined urban sample population status shows that out of a total population size of 236, the number of individual using computers and also having Internet experience are 90 and 91 respectively, i.e., 38 per cent. The number of computers available in the total sample families is only 22.

As compared to the urban scenario, the amenability of the rural sample population is poor. In a population of 334, number of people using the computer and Internet is limited to 22, i.e., 0.07 per cent, and another 22 in the use of Internet. On the other hand, the number of people using computers is seven, i.e., 0.01 per cent. Thus the familiarity of rural Delhi with computer and internet is alarmingly low as compared to even the suburban Delhi.

The pattern of familiarity with computer and Internet across the social strata in the rural areas of Delhi indicates that out of 112 general categories population only 11, i.e., 10 per cent, persons each know use of computers and that of Internet, and enjoy possession of personal computers. Similarly out of the SC population of 80 only nine persons use computers and are familiar with the Internet. This is a miserably low figure. As regards the OBC sample segment, it came out that in a population of 142 that only two persons each are familiar with the use of computers and Internet. These figures compare very poorly with both the general category and the SC category population.

The overall position regarding familiarity with computers and Internet, and possession of personal computers indicates that in a population of 570, Delhi's number of people with computer acquaintance is 113 and only 29 families own personal computers.

The Content Pattern

The study also captured the preference pattern of the sample population in their most commonly available digital world-conducive facility of cable or satellite-based television broadcasting. The objective was to ascertain as to what kind of content has been the favourite of the viewers. The survey data revealed that invariably in all socio-economic and spatial categories cable/satellite television is sought for entertainment and information content. This reveals that digital content has to be more focused on providing entertainment content mainly, followed by information and education. The majority of 570 population in the sample areas indicated that families prefer entertainment material. Please see Annexure 6.

Digital Conduciveness Analysis

Since the analysis of socio-economic and spatial-strata wise position of computing facilities, communication facilities and content preferences, as detailed in the preceding sections, does not clearly indicate a combined statement on the preparedness of the families to shift from the present IT, ICT and broadcasting paradigm to the digital convergence technology era, I have constructed a 10-point scale based on simple weights assigned to various computing, communication, content and familiarity indicators, such as availability of cable/satellite, mobile, telephone connectivity; and availability of computers, and finally familiarity with computers and Internet. In this system, familiarity with computers, emails/internet, and possession of computers are assigned a weight of two points each, while all other items 1 point each. The weight for familiarity with computer, familiarity with the Internet, and possession of computer is two points each, irrespective of the numbers indicating these items. For example, even if there are four users of e-mail in a family the weight will remain two only. As regards others, the availability of the facilities as cable/satellite, or telephone or mobile, and the use of content, a weight of 1 each is calculated.

This has the advantage of arriving at a single indicator for each family, each social, and income and spatial group. The utility of this scale lies in providing us a precise assessment of the sample population's status in the present multi-casting scenario wherein both analogue and digital broadcasting and other services are available. Besides this, this indicator would help us form a view on the future ability to shift to digital IT. Now, let us begin with the social strata aggregates to have a macro perspective of the scenario. The sample population of 570 attained a score of 6.3 on the scale. This score signifies the availability of 71 cable/satellite connection, 75 mobiles, 71 telephones, 29 computers, and 113 persons with familiarity with computers and the Internet.

This has an interesting social, economic and spatial strata-wide distribution among General, SC and OBC families and across urban, suburban and rural areas of Delhi. First, among the urban South Delhi sample families, the general category families scored 9.8 points on this scale. This signifies a high degree of adaptability to digital technology. On the other hand, the SC segment scored 6 points. The OBC segment of the South Delhi sample families scored a high 9.8. This means most of the sample families have

Table 1: Social Strata-wise IT-Conduciveness

Social Strata	*No. of Families*	*Communication Links*			*PC availability, familiarity and Internet acquaintance*			*Entertain-ment*	*Score on*
		Cable/Sat TV Weight 1	*Mobile Weight 1*	*Tele. Weight 1*	*Comp. familiar Weight 2*	*Email/Tran-saction Weight 2*	*PC Weight 2*	*Weight 1*	*Scale*
				Urban: South Delhi					
		1	1	1	2	2	2	1	10.0
GC	10	10	10	10	20	20	7	10	9.10
SC	2	1	2	1	3	5	1	1	6.00
OBC	6	5	3	5	12	12	5	5	8.80
Total	18	15	15	15	38	38	13	16	7.97
				Suburban: Panjabi Basti					
GC	12	12	10	12	42	42	5	12	8.90
SC	10	8	7	8	7	7	3	9	5.40
OBC	6	5	5	5	3	4	1	5	5.20
Total	28	25	22	25	52	41	9	26	6.50
Total Urban	46	40	37	40	90	91	22	41	7.24

(Contd...)

(Contd...)

Social Strata	*No. of Families*	*Communication Links*			*PC availability, familiarity and Internet acquaintance*			*Entertain-ment*	*Score on*
		Cable/Sat TV Weight 1	*Mobile Weight 1*	*Tele. Weight 1*	*Comp. familiar Weight 2*	*Email/Tran-saction Weight 2*	*PC Weight 2*	*Weight 1*	*Scale*
Rural: Mukund Pur village									
GC	18	11	7	11	11	11	4	18	4.60
SC	14	10	10	10	9	9	1	14	4.40
OBC	23	23	21	23	2	2	2	24	4.20
Mukund Pur									
	55	31	38	31	22	22	7	56	5.00
Overall Delhi									
Grand Total	100	71	75	71	113	113	29	97	6.12

The additions vertically show total numbers, and horizontal additions of the weights given to each family/category. The category wise and grand total scores are simple averages of the individual weight scores. Category wise score on the scale is simple average of total score of the category as shown in Annexure 1. The Spatial Division scores are simple averages of the social category/sub-spatial averages as given in this table.

GC:General Category SC: Scheduled Caste, OBC: Other Backward Castes.

crucial connectivities, and computing back up, along with familiarity with the computers and the Internet. The advantage of the locality, being a village surviving as an island of villagers in the teeming South Delhi urban life under the existing land rights, it enjoys the best urban amenities.

This pattern of conduciveness across the social segments indicates that in the urban areas the difference may limit to only possession of computers and familiarity, all other infostructure requirements are generally fulfilled.

In the spatial set-up of suburban Punjabi Basti area, near Delhi University, the situation is different. It is a colony of displaced erstwhile Pakistani Hindu Punjabis, migrants from rural areas of neighbouring states, Tibetans and Nepalis. It is 18 kilometres away from the heart of South Delhi. Engaged in various low-profile livelihood earning jobs, small business and servicing the main city, it is a typical suburban area.

The sample of 28 families with 153 population scored 6.5 points on the scale. This 2.9 difference from the South Delhi sample signifies a serious disadvantage in the pattern of familiarity with computers and Internet, and possession of computers. For example, whereas South Delhi's 80 per cent families met cent-per-cent conditions on all accounts, in Punjabi Basti, only 52 persons knew how to use computer and the Internet, and nine families had computers, indicating 34 per cent of the population of 153, and only 32 per cent of 28 families.

The general category families in Punjabi Basti scored 8.9, the SC families 5.4 per cent, and the OBC sample families scored 5.1 per cent. This break-up for the three category indicates that the general category sample families stood much lower on the scale as compared to their South Delhi counterparts, and so did the SC and OBC families as compared to their urban counterparts. More importantly the difference is in the more mattering area of familiarity with computers and Internet, and availability of computers.

When we go to the typical rural area, away from the sub-urban Delhi, the pattern that emerges is entirely different. Now we see, the combined score of the 56 family sample, with a population of 334, is only 5.0, which compares very poorly with the urban Delhi, and adversely with the suburban one. This score suggests that the majority of these families meet only basic conditions of communication connections, and one of the two familiarity criteria or possession of a computer. Of the total sample families and population, the general category scored 4.6, the SC 4.5, and the OBC 4.2 points on the scale.

On the basis of this 10-point scale, the picture that emerges about availability of communication facilities, computing facilities, and familiarity of the people with computers and Internet, and content preference is as follows:

1. In the urban population, 80 per cent general category families attained 10 points in the 10-point scale. This means these families meet all major computing, communication and content attributes of a digital-conducive status. The remaining 20 per cent score 5 to 6 points.
2. Among the SC families of urban Delhi the attainment of attributes is between 3 and 5.
3. The OBC families also score 10 points of attainment in 80 per cent of their population in the urban Delhi, and 6 points in the remaining 20 per cent.

When the position of suburban Delhi is probed with this 10-point test of digital-conduciveness, the following results were found:

1. Six out of 12 families among the general category population enjoyed 10 points in the scale, indicating that all three 'Cs' were available in these families. The remaining families stand between 5 and 6 points on the scale. This means roughly 50 per cent families met the digital-conduciveness test completely, while the rest scored less.
2. Among the SC sample population segment only three families out of the total 10 scored 8 points in the scale, while others scored between 3 and 8 points. This indicates that only 30 per cent families qualify the digital-conduciveness test substantially, while others remain far below.
3. In the same way only two OBC families could score 6 points in the scale, and the others remained between 3 and 4 points. This indicates only 40 per cent OBC families in a digital-conducive status.

The digital-conduciveness scale analysis of rural population highlights the following points:

1. Only one family out of the general category sample families, numbering 18, scored 10 points, while two others could reach 6 points on the scale. The rest of sample families, 11 families, fall between 2 and 5 points. This means that the majority of general category families scores very poorly on the digital-conduciveness scale.
2. As regards SC sample families only one out of 14 families scored 10 points, while the others remain mainly between 1 and 4 points and still others between 4 and 6 points.
3. The OBC sample families, numbering 24, scored between 2 and 4 in the majority of the sample population, with an exception of 6 points and 5 points scored by 2 families. This means only about 4 per cent families were close to digital-conduciveness score of 10, while others, around 96 per cent, stood very low in the scale.

Literacy and Digital Conduciveness

Literacy rate substantially influences the degree of digital or IT-conduciveness among people. But the extent of this influence on various social, economic and spatial strata must be ascertained by meticulously analysing this tendency. This will help in determining the gaps that exist purely on account of the literacy level and to establish whether literacy is a factor that plays a role bigger than the economic status and spatial advantages do.

It is considered that for acquainting with computers and Internet, and learn professional skills of various levels, one has to be a matriculate at least even though computer skills can be learnt by people with much lower educational qualification. The educational attainments recorded in the survey data is for matriculate and above including postgraduate degrees. The normal literacy figures might not have served the purpose of this study. To relate digital/IT-conduciveness to a family's educational attainments, families of various socio-economic strata were assessed on the 10-point scale. (See Table 2 and Annexure 4.)

The relationship between educational attainments and the levels of digital or IT conduciveness of an individual or the family

Table 2. Literacy and Strata Socio-economic and Rural-Urban Digital-Conduciveness

Social Strata/Familie	*Popu-lations*	*Communication*			*Users*		*Content*		*Score on*
		Cable/Sat TV Weight 1	*Mob Weight 1*	*Tele Weight 1*	*Comp familiar Weight 2*	*Email/Tran-saction Weight 2*	*Entertain ment/info Weight 1*	*PC Weight 2*	*10 point Scale*
		1	1	1	2	2	1	2	10.00
GC	46	10	10	10	20	20	10	7	9.10
SC	8	1	2	1	3	5	1	1	6.00
OBC	29	5	3	5	12	12	5	5	8.80
S Delhi	83	15	15	15	38	38	16	13	7.97
Gc	56	12	10	12	42	42	12	5	8.90
SC	63	8	7	8	7	7	9	3	5.40
OBC	34	5	5	5	3	4	5	1	5.20
Punjabi Basti	153	25	22	25	52	41	26	9	6.50
Urban	236	40	37	40	90	91	41	22	7.24
GC	112	11	7	11	11	11	18	4	4.60
SC	80	10	10	10	9	9	14	1	4.40
OBC	142	23	21	23	2	2	24	2	4.20
Mukund Pur	334	31	38	31	22	22	56	7	5.00
Grand Total	570	71	75	71	113	113	97	29	6.12

The additions vertically show total numbers, and horizontal additions of the weights given to each family/category. The category-wise and grand total scores are simple averages of the individual weight scores. Category-wise score on the scale is simple average of total score of the category as shown in Annexure 1. The Spatial Division scores are simple averages of the social category/sub-spatial averages as given in this table.

GC:General Category SC: Scheduled Caste, OBC: Other Backward Castes.

can be seen with reference to the spatial location and social strata. On the total sample level, it is found that one of the major determinant of 6.3 scale was the educational level. The number of matriculation and above in the 570 sample population was 130, indicating 22.8 per cent. In other words low conduciveness scores have more to do with education than the economic status.

In the sample population, the urban population of South Delhi with a matriculation and above literate population of 57 per cent, the conduciveness score for general category is 9, with a perfect 10 score in 80 per cent cases; 6 for SC segment, and 9.8 for OBC. The matriculation and above literacy figure for general category is 60 per cent, for SC families 75 per cent, and for OBC only 45 per cent. Interestingly the higher score of 9.8 in the case of OBC is a result of not so low literate population, and predominance of the sample by high income strata.

The suburban population of Delhi, with a matriculation and above literate persons percentage of 38 per cent, has a digital/IT-conduciveness score of 6.9. The general category in this sample area has 36 per cent defined literacy and has a score of 8.9, and SC sample families with 21 per cent defined literacy has a score of 5.4, and the OBC sample families with a 6.33 per cent literacy had a lower score of 5.1.

The urban sample population as a whole, with 38 per cent of the population with matriculation and above education, has a score of 7.65.

But the rural sample area, with low educational level of 22.8 per cent matriculation and above literacy and predominance of middle and poor income people in all the three categories, the conduciveness score is as low as 5. This simply means that an overwhelming majority of these village folks simply do not have computing facilities, communication links, and familiarity with computers and Internet.

Content Use Pattern

The data collected on content is about the major use of cable/satellite. It reveals, without any exception, that people in all social, economic categories and spatial groupings use cable/satellite links for entertaining themselves, except in a few cases wherein the art of life stuff is watched. Another area of interest in content is information. Many individuals in the sample size showed their interest in spirituality and yoga.

Priority

Where does the computer stand in the priority list of Delhi's people? The survey tried to find it out. The survey captured data on possession of such assets as TV, car, motorcycle or scooter and mobile to correlate this set of lifestyle assets to owning a PC, and use of computers and the Internet.

In the sample population 29 families were found owning PC, and also familiar with their use and the Internet. Out of these 10 families were from South Delhi sample population. Among these only two families had TV, car, mobike and mobile. All of them had TV and mobiles, while four families had cars. This indicates that people tend to own a priority that places it after TV and mobike, but before car. In all the remaining cases generally those who own a TV, car, mobike and mobile also tend to own a computer, while many families may own all other things except a computer.

Perception of IT Future

The respondents were asked to reflect on the future of IT or digital economy as per their own perception. The reply was framed to be a bright future, little future or no future. The data gathered from the survey indicate that except for a few respondents, who saw little or no future, the majority were convinced of a very bright future.

The Digital Reach

The respondents were also enquired about their views on enabling IT and ICT reach in every house and every corner of the country.

The replies are summarised below:

1. Most of the family heads and other members viewed that rural education system should be used for propagating computer/IT. It emerged from queries that rural education with full computer teaching provision would solve the problem of economic and other handicaps.
2. Another frequently suggested point by the sampled population was bringing down computer hardware prices so that it was affordable to all economic sections.
3. Most of the respondents thought that penetration of IT skills in the rural areas and among the poor segments of

population would be possible only by making IT and multimedia learning available in the rural schools, and by opening IT educational institution in the rural areas.

4. Many interviewees, including professionals working in corporate sectors, pointed out that IT and IT skills awareness can be generated by special awareness workshops, and training to the rural population, and to special learning target groups.

6

Conclusion

Just as digitalisation and converging technologies have led to the birth of new economy in the advanced countries, so the spectacular emergence of the IT sector in India has made her a strong contender for prominence as a new world economy. But the digital technology did not come without problems of its own for the world economy. The global scenario was marked with a visible gap between its development in the most advanced and advanced countries, and still more gaping was the hiatus between countries of the advanced world and the developing one. But the issue of dichotomy doesn't end here. The countries just stepping into the threshold of digital economy have much more to worry about it.

6.1. Beyond Global Digital Divide

Beyond the global digital divide concerns of the international developmental gaps, countries like India need to investigate carefully the nature and extent of social and spatial inequalities in the development of information communication technology in its digital avatar. The Indian socio-economic and spatial inequality scenario, with its dehumanising social, economic and location disadvantages, makes it necessary to assess the present status and evaluate the plan and policy prescriptions in view of the emerging trends.

This necessitates examination of the content and extent of global digitalisation and technological convergence leading to the digital world economy; the Eleventh Plan thrust to mitigate social and spatial divide in digital development; and finally, understanding and appraising the conduciveness of the present rural and urban masses in their leap into the new world economy.

6.2. Global Digital Economy

A survey of the global economy of today brings out the fact that with the technological leap to new digital technology, the economies of the world have undergone a transformation characterised by digital technology, micro processors, servers, computing information, information high way, multimedia and intelligent networking.

The global economies now run on new concepts and themes which shape the nature of solutions to all economic and management problems. These concepts and themes include knowledge-based solutions, digitisation of all processes, virtual solutions, molecular operational scale, disintermediation, convergence in technology, leaders led innovations, presumptions, immediacy, globalisation and discordance. These themes and concepts being the underlying basis for digital economy's way of working, nature of digital economies is bound to be startling.

The internetworked economy, according to Don Tapscott's studies, has shifted corporate focus from growth through technological and managerial excellence to growth through wealth and business creation, through value additions. This wealth generation happens through a multilayered transformation. It begins with the Effective Individual who, equipped with multimedia and assigned with the task of efficiency and excellence, is able to act, update, access, consult, advice and test ideas fast. This layer is linked to the next, i.e., the High Performance Team which, equipped with the group competition facilities and assigned with the task of business processes and strategy designing, guides the Effective Individual by responding faster to the business environment, by bringing resources together. The third layer is that of Integrated Organisation which, equipped with enterprise infostructure and assigned with the task of effective supervision, interacts with the High Performance Team by focusing on business applications, information and technology, and world corporate cohesiveness.

The fourth layer is Extended Enterprise which, equipped with enterprise infostructure and with the objective of recasting external relationship, interacts with outside organisations, information being generated by all corporate bodies. The topmost layer, i.e., the fifth one, is Integrated Internetworked Enterprise with worldwide connectivity through the net, and focuses on wealth creation and social development.

Internetworked Sectors of the Global Economy

One of the major areas of internetworked economies is news media and entertainment. With the arrival of digital technology, a revolution has come in the news media and entertainment business in the industry. The entire world is moving fast to the digital mode in all stages of production, distribution, sales and management. Another area going internetworked is governance and learning. All countries of the world have entered the era of virtualisation of several important functions that the government were performed as its fundamental responsibility to the citizens.

6.3. Digital Global Economy Problems

But the global digital economy is facing teething problems. Major problems are related to employment, particularly about downsizing of the clerical and professional manpower due to virtualisation and molecularisation, effects of technological convergence on more employment, the opportunity driving many players to less developed countries; decline in the old economy jobs; and upsurge in high skill jobs; the effects of delinking of work from physical presence on a social relationship. Other issues are access to and equity in information and technology; income and equity issues; inherent adverse effects on the quality of life; electronic democracy and polity, and metro-economy and nations state.

But when we talk of transforming India into a new world digital economy what it implies is a development that brings into its fold the entire society, spaces and resources. It really implies including not only rural areas and less developed urban segment, but also the socially and economically fringed lots.

6.4. India's Plan Agenda

Indian economy is found on a weak footing despite a laudable IT spread strategy for the rural and social disadvantaged.

The highlight of Eleventh Plan IT intervention lies in its aggregate investment of Rs. 87,745 crores in three departments, namely, the Department of Information Technology, Telecommunication, and Information and Broadcasting. Second, this strategy has elaborate plans for enabling IT penetration right up to the village schools and poor quarters of the society. Third, its programmes are well-experienced in their approach and conception.

Already India has become a premier IT and IT-enabled service sourcing destination, and much more is in the offing. The New Economy has become a standard for this realisation of the endless benefits that can accrue to a society due to information technology's conduciveness in attaining excellence in production, distribution and management; and evolving entirely new concepts of production, services, management and product designs.

The Eleventh Five Year Plan debate, as evident from Working Group and Steering Committee reports and discussions, and the final plan documents, has necessitated the need for gearing up Indian economy for much higher growth, but without overlooking the need for inclusive approach towards development. In the Eleventh Five Year Plan, IT and IT-enabled services related talent promotion has been focused on both in the short-run and long-run perspectives. Schemes for encouraging development of IT talents have been developed at the schooling level, and also at the graduate level: by bringing in the concept of finishing schools for topping up skills at the school level; introducing bridge courses for mid-level managers; and by expansion of Masters and Doctors programme in IT, health care, transportation, manufacturing, nanotechnology, and animation and entertainment.

Similarly in the telecom sector, the present planning focus is on rural telephony which has emerged as a thrust area for ensuring growth in rural economy. Another area of clear priority is broadband coverage in secondary and higher secondary schools, public health care centre, gram panchayat, and State Wide Area Network (SWAN).

A massive virtual skill development resource networking for training people at doorsteps targeting at 10 million people during the Eleventh Plan was conceived. Designed to execute through 50,000 Skill Development Centres, this scheme would be implemented with the involvement of the Department if Information Technology, Micro, Small, and Medium Enterprises, and Ministry of Textiles.

But the most important developmental move for the rural areas, the socio-economically and geographically fringed strata and areas, has come from the massive plan for digitalisation of the public service broadcasting, Prasar Bharati, with its Doordarshan and All India Radio wings. In addition to this, information and film media units of Ministry of Information and Broadcasting too have taken significant policy decisions towards promoting human skills in such areas as gaming and animation.

The significance of digitalising government's public service media units of information and broadcasting lies in its vital function of making the public aware of social, economic, cultural developments; and nurturing a healthy and responsible social outlook among the people. The government-owned media units, handling publicity, information, film and theatre, accomplish the twin task of informing and educating through entertainment. Social, economic and cultural promotional goals within and without the country, and building better international relationship are the major goals of the pubic service media units.

Even though the :nerging planning priorities are based on both global digital economy experience and issues, and India's own experience of high growth in the IT sector, what is required is to make a massive plan move towards enabling the socio-economically and spatially fringed segments overcome their economic, literacy and locational handicaps. Instead of depending on far-fetched reasoning that eventually developmental benefit would reach the poor and the disadvantaged, the country needs to think of practical ways and means to equip everybody with a minimum skill required to enjoy the digital economy benefits.

But what the Indian plan lacks seriously is in its perception of ground realities. Given the slow pace of development of transport and communications means, persistent illiteracy and poverty in rural India, particularly amongst the disadvantaged hilly, deserts and forests state, the programmes conceived are likely to suffer setbacks in achieving the goals.

Our grand developmental strategy is left at the mercy of an inadequate monitoring mechanism, and a machinery carved out of skeletal government manpower. The funding agencies in the government, the Union Planning Commission, the State Planning Commissions, have literally left monitoring and implementation on low priority, limiting themselves to an 'uncommitted quarterly or half-yearly progress reviews. This is a deplorable situation; if one looks at the poor, only close to 50 per cent find utilisation during the Tenth Plan, financial and physical performance, and miserable implementation record of a large number of the projects.

One must acknowledge that a serious monitoring of the implementation of the projects would go a long way in improving plan implementation. PMGSY, a successful rural road connectivity scheme with record speed and high quality roads, is a justification for taking implementation monitoring in a big way. PMGSY's results are mainly attributed to its rather over-monitoring feature. It was monitored on four levels: national, state, district and project operation. Even though criticised for excess monitoring, poor performance of majority of or high priority projects only justify replication of the PMGSY model.

It is here that the need for assessing the IT and digital development conduciveness of the country's disadvantaged lot becomes all the more important. Let us see the findings of the case study as produced in the brief given in the following section.

6.5. Preparedness for Digital Leap

In the face of global digital economy realities and India's impressive IT development, assessing the IT and digital-preparedness of the country's disadvantaged lot becomes all the more important.

My case study of Delhi reveals interesting aspects of the digital disparity issue. On the 10-point digital IT conduciveness scale, various socio-economic and spatial strata of Delhi have found themselves in sharp variations.

Urban Areas

First, in the urban population of South Delhi, 80 per cent general category families attained 10 points, meaning that the people are fully geared up for a leap to a digital world economy. This implies that these families meet all major computing, communication and content conditions for digitalisation. The remaining 20 per cent are half way in their conduciveness towards digitalisation. Second, the SC families of urban Delhi are far behind in their attainment of attributes conducive to digitalisation. They scored between 5 and 6 points on the scale. Third, among the OBC sample families, 80 per cent scored 9.8 points, and the remaining population scored six points. This places them on a very comfortable position vis-à-vis other segments. The location advantage of having their habitat in the heart of the South Delhi, and sound economic conditions have contributed to their high score in the scale.

Suburban Areas

In the suburban Delhi of Punjabi Basti, the conduciveness of the population to digitalisation indicated, first, six out of 12 families among the general category population scored 10 points, indicating that all three 'Cs' were available in these families. The remaining families stand between 5 and 6 points in the scale. This means roughly 50 per cent families are comfortable in their journey towards digitalisation, while the rest are off the mark.

Second, among the SC sample population only three families out of the total 10 scored 8 points in the scale, while others scored between 3 and 8 points. This indicates that only 30 per cent meet 80 per cent conditions for shift to digital world economy where availability of all computing, communication and content facilities are available, while others remain far below. Third, among the OBC segment, only two OBC families could score 6 points in the scale, and the others remained between 3 and 4 points. This indicates that only 40 per cent OBC families meet digital-conduciveness conditions.

Rural Areas

The digital-conduciveness scale analysis of Delhi's rural population highlights that, first, only one family out of the general category sample families, numbering 18, scored 10 points, while two others could reach 6 points in the scale. The rest, 11 families, fall between 2 and 5 points. This means that the majority of the general category families scored very low on the digital-conduciveness scale. This implies that in the village, even in a state as advanced as Delhi, a majority of the population is far away from meeting even the minimum conditions for an easy shift to digital economy. Even a Delhi village lacks communication facilities, computing means and content availability. Second, as regards the SC sample families, only one out of 14 families scored 10 points, while others remained mainly between 1 and 4 points and still others between 4 and 6 points. The digital-conduciveness among the Scheduled Caste families in rural Delhi appears to be the lowest. Almost the entire sample segment falls in the very poor score category segment. Both on communication links and computing facilities, these families lie in a disadvantageous position.

Third, the OBC sample families, numbering 23, scored between 2 and 4 in the majority of the sample population. It means that only about 4 per cent families are close to digital-conduciveness score of 10, while others, around 96 per cent, stood very low in the scale.

Literacy and Income level

Literacy appears to be the key determinant of digital conduciveness because it influences various socio-economic and spatial factors in a big way. Education as the major determinant appeared to have played a role in keeping the total sample population's digital conduciveness score at a low level of 6.3 points. The number of matriculation and above qualification in the 570 sample population was 130, indicating 22.8 per cent.

Low conduciveness scores have more to do with education than economic status. This is evident from the social strata and literacy positions. First, the urban population of South Delhi with a matriculation and above literate population of 57 per cent scored 9 points in the general category, with a perfect 10 score in 80 per cent cases; 6 points in SC segment, and 9.8 for OBC. Second, the suburban population of Delhi with a matriculation and above literacy percentage of 38 per cent has a digital/IT-conduciveness score of 6.9. The general category in this sample area has 36 per cent defined literacy and has a score of 8.9, and SC sample families with 21% defined literacy has a score of 5.4, and the OBC sample families with 6.33 per cent literacy had a lower score of 5.1. The urban sample population with 38 per cent matriculation and above literacy scored 7.65 points on the scale. Third, the rural sample with 22.8 per cent matriculation and above literacy, and predominance of middle and poor income families in all the three categories, scored as low as 5 points. This means an overwhelming majority of these village folks simply do not have computing facilities, communication links and familiarity with the computers and Internet.

6.6. Findings of the Case Study

First, the economic, literacy and spatial status of an individual or a family, or a social category determine digital and IT conduciveness in Indian scenario. This is because of limited availability or complete non-availability of learning opportunities specifically meant for improving IT skills beyond one's own personal infostructure.

Second, among the three handicaps, poverty, illiteracy and disadvantageous locations, illiteracy is the biggest handicap. Economic handicap may disable an individual to own infostructure, but one is able to overcome computer illiteracy by using public or private facilities available.

Third, it has emerged from discussions with the interviewees that only an effective school-level IT education for the disadvantage masses can improve their future prospects of getting into the digital economy race. This is true of the government's rural and urban schools.

Fourth, this handicap, as suggested by many sample families, can be overcome to a great extent by organising awareness programmes and workshops in the rural areas, and by opening rural IT learning institutions. This needs special focus on skill development.

Fifth, the government can even provide public private partnership based free rural learning centres for encouraging the rural people to use IT and IT-enabled systems of day-to-day needs, and to move towards more learning.

Table 3. Income Strata-wise IT-Conduciveness

Strata (No. of Families)	*% of Families with High Income*	*Communication Links*			*PC Availability, Familiarity, and Internet-Acquaintance*			*Entertain-ment*	*Score on 10 point Scale*
		Cable/Sat TV Weight 1	*Mob Weight 1*	*Tele Weight 1*	*Comp-familiar Weight 2*	*Email/Tran-saction Weight 2*	*PC Weight 2*	*Weight 1*	
				Urban: South Delhi					
		1	1	1	2	2	2	1	10.00
G C (10)	46	10	10	10	20	20	7	10	9.10
SC (2)	8	1	2	1	3	5	1	1	6.00
OBC (6)	29	5	3	5	12	12	5	5	8.80
Total (17)	83	15	15	15	38	38	13	16	7.97
				Suburban: Punjabi Basti					
GC (12)	56	12	10	12	42	42	5	12	8.90
SC (10)	63	8	7	8	7	7	3	9	5.40
OBC (6)	34	5	5	5	3	4	1	5	5.20
Total (28)	153	25	22	25	52	41	9	26	6.50
Total Urban 45	236	40	37	40	90	91	22	41	7.24
				Rural: Mukund Pur Village					
GC (18)	112	11	7	11	11	11	4	18	4.60
SC (14)	80	10	10	10	9	9	1	14	4.40
OBC (24)	142	23	21	23	2	2	2	24	4.20
Mukund Pur (56)	334	31	38	31	22	22	7	56	5.00
				Overall Delhi					
Grand Total	570	71	75	71	113	113	29	97	6.12

Sixth, the study reveals, without any exception, that people in all social, economic categories and spatial groupings use cable/ satellite connectivity for entertaining themselves, or, once in a while, for the art of life, information, spirituality and yoga.

Seventh, in the priority list of Delhi's people personal computer and internet connections come after acquiring a TV and mobike, but before buying a car. Generally those who own a TV, a car, a mobike and a mobile, may tend to own a computer, while many families may own all of these durables except a computer.

Eighth, the future of IT or digital economy in people's perception, in terms of a bright future, little future or no future, is very bright in view of the majority of the respondents.

Ninth, suggestions from the respondents regarding reach and penetration of IT and digital activities and opportunities indicate that people feel strongly for effectiveness of such steps as providing rural schools with computing and connectivity facilities; bringing down computer hardware and connectivity prices; by opening IT training institutions in rural areas; and finally by conducting special awareness workshop and training courses focused on skill development.

6.7. Policy Prescriptions

New policy prescriptions are needed for tackling global digital economy realities of techno-economic moorings, and India's own socio-economic and technological dynamics. The challenge lies in finding the right solutions to all the techno-economic issues of global nature so that the world experience is synthesized in the vibrant Indian economy's ICT strength, while insulating the susceptible socio-economic fabric of India against any strains and pains.

The policy focus should be on the following issues:

1. For ensuring a balanced development of digital economy in India, the Eleventh Plan package for rural area's IT and digital skilled development and investment should be effectively monitored and implemented in the line of PMGSY scheme of rural roads. Close and effective monitoring alone can ensure reach of the golden fraction of resources to the rural target in absence of public cognisance of government affairs.

2. Programmes focusing on IT education of school, college and postgraduate levels have to be given top priority. This needs to be done simultaneously with massive IT skill development programme monitoring and review. The One Laptop Per Child vision for India got shot down in the typical politico-bureaucratic crossfires more motivated by the age-old Indian zeal for playing down or opposing everything happening and optimistic. Policy makers who see laptops as 'detrimental to the growth of creative and analytical abilities of the child' are oblivious of both how their grandchildren are growing and are alien to the Internet and digital world's potentials. What is required is computer labs in every school for all three levels—primary, middle and senior, schools.
3. Not only the rural disadvantaged population but the urban and suburban poor and socially and educationally backward segments need a package for facilitating their IT development. The sub-urban population is at a great disadvantage as a whole, but the backward sections are in far more disadvantaged state.
4. Since economic unaffordability and illiteracy are two major factors responsible for non-preparedness for a digital leap in rural and suburban areas, strengthening public access to IT facilities through skilled development centres, and massive IT-orientation of the government school network should be given thrust under the plans. Even though the Eleventh Five Year Plans stress on IT and ITES (IT-enabled services) is laudable, what the implementing agencies have to be concerned about is sluggish and ineffective implementation, which is far less tolerable in an industry which is swift in change in terms of both technology and cost structures.
5. Involvement of the NGO's and public schools for skill development in IT sector and organisation support, and using public private partnership (PPP) as funding, managerial and operational mechanisms can be the solution for organisational and funding issues.
6. The planning and developmental experience so far testify the fallacy of the trickle-down theory. Without effective

and elaborate planning and policy prescriptions, the rural and the urban poor and the socio-economic handicaped would be left waiting for a miracle to improve their social and economic status and their literacy rates, and bring down the prices of computing, communication and content facilities to their levels of affordability. This would leave a huge segment of our population literally with no skill relevance to the fast changing new world economy.

7. Considering the population vision of the Eleventh Plan that very soon India would be facing a decline in the supply of workforce due to a marked decline in the birth rates during last several decades, India needs to give thrust to the digital world economy skill development among the socio-economically and spatially disadvantaged communities.
8. Development of infrastructure in telecom and IT sectors has a huge target of reaching 600 million subscribers (with 200 million rural subscribers) and 20 million broadband and 40 million internet subscribers. The Eleventh Five Year Plan centre and state investment target is Rs.2,58,439 crore, as compared to Rs.1,03,365 crore during the Tenth Plan. In this the rural segment has an investment share of Rs.16,000 crore (source page 258 Volume III, Eleventh Plan). The grand target is to connect all villages with telephone and broadband by 2012. To accomplish this task, effective implementation, and close monitoring will have to be ensured.
9. Providing for regulatory system, and ensuring effective regulation is a must. With no regulatory authority in communication, broadcasting, cable TV and telecom, and Internet, the digital economy growth in India is running a serious risk in all domains: consumer welfare, investment insecurity, and less than expected growth of digital economy.
10. Since the unprecedented scale of investment in the ICT sector in general, and in the areas of digital divide abridging priorities are likely to face implementational setbacks in terms of slow and ineffective project execution, gearing up of the system for a timely Mid-Term Appraisal of the Eleventh Plan is of crucial importance. In recognition

of the fast changing global digital economy size, content and spread, and emergence of new issues, timely policy intervention strategies should be ready. Going by the present practices, MTA should be completed by the middle of 2010.

ANNEXURES

Annexure 1: Socio-Economic and Spatial Strata and Digital/IT Conduciveness in Delhi

Sl.		Social Category/ Income	Communication Cable/Sat. TV Weight 1	Mob. Weight 1	Tele. Weight 1	User Comp. familiar Weight 2	Email/Tra.-nsaction Weight 2	Content Entertain-ment/info Weight 1	PC Weight 2	Score on 10 point Scale
	1	Gch 6	C	M	T	3	3	E	P	10.00
	2	Gch 4	C	M	T	3	2	E	P	10.00
	3	Gch 4	C	M	T	2	3	E	P	10.00
	4	Gch 3	C	M	T	3	2	E	P	10.00
	5	Gch 5	C	M	T	2	3	E	P	10.00
	6	Gch 6	C	M	T	3	4	E	P	10.00
	7	Gch 6	C	M	T	4	3	E	P	10.00
	8	Gcl 8	C	M	T	3		E	P	10.00
	9	Gcl 2	C	M	T		1	E		6.00
	10	Gcl 2	C	M	T	1		E		5.00
GC		46	10	10	10	20	20	10	7	9.10
	1	Sch 4	C	M	Y	1	3		P	8.00
	2	Sch 4		M			2	Y		4.00
SC		8	1	2	1	3	5	1	1	6.00
	1	Obch 4	C		T	2	3	E	P	9.00
	2	Obch 11	C	M	T	5	3	E	P	10.00
3		Obch 4	C	M	T	3	3	E	P	10.00

(Contd...)

(Contd...)

Sl.		Social Category/ Income	Communication: Cable/Sat. TV Weight 1	Communication: Mob. Weight 1	Communication: Tele. Weight 1	User: Comp. familiar Weight 2	User: Email/Tra.-nsaction Weight 2	Content: Entertain-ment/info Weight 1	PC Weight 2	Score on 10 point Scale
	4	Obch 6	C	M	T	3	2	E	P	10.00
	5	Obch 4	C		T	2	4	E	P	10.00
	6	OBC L	C	M		2				4.00
OBC		**29**	**5**	**3**	**5**	**12**	**12**	**5**	**5**	**8.80**
S Delhi		**83**	**15**	**15**	**15**	**38**	**38**	**16**	**13**	**7.97**
	1	Gch 4	C	M	T	3	3	E	P	10.00
	2	Gch 6	C	M	T	2	2	E		10.00
	3	Gch 7	C	M	T	3	3	E	P	10.00
	4	Gch 6	C	M	T	2	2	E	P	10.00
	5	Gch 4	C	M	T	1	1	E	P	10.00
	6	Gch 2	C	M	T	2	2	E	P	10.00
	7	Gch 3	C		T	5	5	E		7.00
	8	Gcl 4	C	M	T	4	4	E		8.00
	9	Gcl 4	C	M	T	4	4	E		8.00
	10	Gcl 4	C		T	4	4	E		8.00
	11	Gcl 6	C	M	T	6	6	E		8.00

(Contd...)

(Contd...)

			Communication			User		Content		Score
Sl.		Social Category/ Income	Cable/Sat. TV Weight 1	Mob. Weight 1	Tele. Weight 1	Comp. familiar Weight 2	Email/Tra-nsaction Weight 2	Entertain-ment/info Weight 1	PC Weight 2	on 10 point Scale
	12	Gcl 6	C		T	6	6	E		8.00
GC		**56**	**12**	**10**	**12**	**42**	**42**	**12**	**5**	**8.9**
	1	Sch1 1	C	M	T		2	E		6.00
	2	Scm 6		M				E	P	4.00
	3	Scm 8	C	M	T		2	E	P	8.00
	4	Scm 5	C	M	T	2	1	E		8.00
	5	Scl 6	C	M	T			E		4.00
	6	Scl 6	C	M	T	2	2	E		8.00
	7	Scl 7	C		T	1		E		5.00
	8	Scl 6	C		T			E		3.00
	9	Scl 3	C		T	2		E	P	7.00
	10	Scl 5		M						1.00
SC	**63**	**8**	**7**	**8**	**7**	**7**	**9**	**3**	**5.4**	
	1	Obch 5	C	M	T			Y		4.00
	2	Obcm 5	C		T			Y		3.00
	3	Obcl 5	C	M	T		1	Y	P	8.00

(Contd...)

(Contd...)

Sl.	*Social Category/ Income*	*Communication*			*User*		*Content*		*Score*
		Cable/Sat. TV Weight 1	*Mob. Weight 1*	*Tele. Weight 1*	*Comp. familiar Weight 2*	*Email/Tra.-nsaction Weight 2*	*Entertain-ment/info Weight 1*	*PC Weight 2*	*on 10 point Scale*
4	Obcl 6	C	M	T	1	2	Y		8.00
5	Obcl 5	C		T	2		Y		5.00
6	Obcl 8	C		T			Y		3.00
OBC	**34**	**5**	**5**	**5**	**3**	**4**	**5**	**1**	**5.20**
Panjabi Basti	**153**	**25**	**22**	**25**	**52**	**41**	**26**	**9**	**6.50**
Urban	**236**	**40**	**37**	**40**	**90**	**91**	**41**	**22**	**7.24**
1	Gch 5	C		T	1		E	P	6.00
2	Gcl 7				1		E		3.00
3	Gcl 5	C		T		1	E		4.00
4	Gcl 6	C		T	1	1	E		7.00
5	Gcl 4	C	M	T	3		E	P	8.00
6	Gcl 4		M			1	E		4.00
7	Gcl 6					3	E	P	5.00
8	Gcl 4	C		T			E		3.00

(Contd...)

(Contd...)

Sl.		Social Category/ Income	Communication			User		Content		Score
			Cable/Sat. TV Weight 1	Mob. Weight 1	Tele. Weight 1	Comp. familiar Weight 2	Email/Tra.-nsaction Weight 2	Entertain-ment/info Weight 1	PC Weight 2	on 10 point Scale
	9	Gcl 5	C		T			E		3.00
	10	Gcl 5						E		1.00
	11	Gck 5		M				E		2.00
	12	Gcl 9	C	M	T			E		4.00
	13	Gcl 6	C	M	T	1	1	E		7.00
	14	Gcl 7	C	M	T	3	3	E	p	10.00
	15	Gcl 6	C					E		2.00
	16	Gcl 5	C		T	1	1	E		5.00
	17	Gcl 8	C		T			E		6.00
	18	1gcl 5	C		T			E		3.00
GC		**112**	**11**	**7**	**11**	**11**	**11**	**18**	**4**	**4.60**
	1	Sch 6	C		T			E		3.00
	2	Scm 6	C	M	T	2	2	E		8.00
	3	Scm 5	C	M	T	2	2	E	P	9.00
	4	Scl 7	C	M	T	2	2	E		6.00
	5	Scl 6	C	M	T			E		4.00

(Contd...)

(Contd...)

Sl.		*Social Category/ Income*	*Communication*			*User*		*Content*		*Score*
			Cable/Sat. TV Weight 1	*Mob. Weight 1*	*Tele. Weight 1*	*Comp. familiar Weight 2*	*Email/Tra.-nsaction Weight 2*	*Entertain-ment/info Weight 1*	*PC Weight 2*	*on 10 point Scale*
	6	Scl 1	C	M	T			E		3.00
	7	Scl 5		M			2			3.00
	8	7sc 1	C	M	T			E		4.00
	9	Scl 4	C	M	T			E		4.00
	10	Scl 7		M				E		2.00
	11	Scl 5	C	M	T	2	1	E		8.00
	12	Scl 6	C	M	T	1		E		6.00
	13	Scl 7						E		
	14	Scl 6		Y				E		2.00
SC		**80**	**10**	**10**	**10**	**9**	**9**	**14**	**1**	**4.40**
	1	Obch 17	C	M	T		1	E	P	7.00
	2	Obcm 8	C	M	T			E		4.00
	3	Obcm 5	C	M	T			E		4.00
	4	Obcm 5	C	M	T			E		4.00

(Contd...)

(Contd...)

Sl.	Social Category/ Income	Communication			User		Content		Score
		Cable/Sat. TV Weight 1	Mob. Weight 1	Tele. Weight 1	Comp. familiar Weight 2	Email/Tra.-nsaction Weight 2	Entertain-ment/info Weight 1	PC Weight 2	on 10 point Scale
5	Obcm 7	C	M	T			E		4.00
6	Obcm 5	C	M	T			E		4.00
7	Obcm 6	C		T	1	2	E	P	6.00
8	Obcm 4	C		T			E		3.00
9	Obcm 7	C	M	T			E		4.00
10	Obcm 7	C	M	T			E		4.00
11	Obcm 7	C	M	T			E		4.00
12	Obcm 4	C	M	T			E		4.00
13	Obcm 8	C		T	2		E		4.00
14	Obcm 8	C	M	T			E		4.00
15	Obcl 7	C	M	T			E		4.00
16	Obcl 4	C	M	T			E		4.00
17	Obcl 6	C	M	T			E		4.00
18	Obcl 6	C	M	T			E		4.00

(Contd...)

(Contd...)

Sl.	Social Category/ Income	Communication			User		Content		Score
		Cable/Sat. TV Weight 1	Mob. Weight 1	Tele. Weight 1	Comp. familiar Weight 2	Email/Tra.-nsaction Weight 2	Entertain-ment/info Weight 1	PC Weight 2	on 10 point Scale
19	Obcl 8	C	M	T			E		4.00
20	Obc l 5	C	M	T			E		4.00
21	Obc l 5	C	M	T			E		4.00
22	Obcl 6	C	M	T			E		4.00
23	Obcl 3	C		T			E		3.00
OBC	**142**	**23**	**21**	**23**	**2**	**2**	**24**	**2**	**4.20**
Mukund Pur	**334**	**31**	**38**	**31**	**22**	**22**	**56**	**7**	**5.00**
Grand Total	**570**	**71**	**75**	**71**	**113**	**113**	**97**	**29**	**6.12**

Note: The Ten point scale is based on a weight of 1 each for positive communication and content reply, 2 each for others: User and PC. The higher the score the more is the family/strata conducive to digital/IT shift. The weight is so calculated as irrespective of quantity of response. For example, for numbers indicating Internet and computer users could be counted as 2, their weights, and the numbers of users.

Also the additions vertically show total numbers, and horizontal additions of the weights give the score. The category-wise and grand total scores are simple averages of the individual scores.

Gch: General category high income, GCM: General Category Middle Income, GLM: General Category Low Income. Similarly, SC (Scheduled Caste and OBC (Other Backward Castes) have been assigned their income groups by suffixing H, M, and L, indicating high, middle, and low income groups as per the incomes defined: Middle Income: Above Rs.2.00 lakhs, Middle Income: between Rs. 1.0 lakhs to Rs. 2.00 lahks; and Low Income: up to Rs.1.00 lakh.

Annexure 2: Literacy and Socio-Economic and Spatial Strata-wise IT Conduciveness in Delhi

Sl.		Category-wise Literates Matric and Above	*Communication*			*User*		*Content*		
			Cable/Sat. TV Weight 1	*Mob. Weight 1*	*Tele. Weight 1*	*Comp-familiar Weight 2*	*Email/Transaction Weight 2*	*Entertainment/info Weight 1*	*PC Weight 2*	*Score on 10 point Scale*
	1	Gch 2	C	M	T	3	3	E	P	10.00
	2	Gch 2	C	M	T	3	2	E	P	10.00
	3	Gch 3	C	M	T	2	3	E	P	10.00
	4	Gch 2	C	M	T	3	2	E	P	10.00
	5	Gch 5	C	M	T	2	3	E	P	10.00
	6	Gch 6	C	M	T	3	4	E	P	10.00
	7	Gch 5	C	M	T	4	3	E	P	10.00
	8	Gcl	C	M	T	3		E	P	10.00
	9	Gcl 1	C	M	T		1	E		6.00
	10	Gcl 2	C	M	T	1		E		5.00
GC	**46**	**10**	**10**	**10**	**20**	**20**	**10**	**7**	**9.1**	
	1	Sch 3	C	M	Y		3		P	8.00
	2	Sch 3		M			2	Y		4.00
SC	**8**	**1**	**2**	**1**	**3**	**5**	**1**	**1**	**6.00**	
	1	Obch 1	C		T	2	**3**	E	P	9.00
	2	Obch 1 6	C	M	T	5	3	E	P	10.00

(Contd...)

(Contd...)

Sl.		Category-wise Literates Matric and Above	Communication			User		Content		Score on 10 point Scale
			Cable/Sat. TV Weight 1	Mob. Weight 1	Tele. Weight 1	Comp-familiar Weight 2	Email/Transaction Weight 2	Entertainment/info Weight 1	PC Weight 2	
	3	Obch 2	C	M	T	3	3	E	P	10.00
	4	Obch 3	C	M	T	3	2	E	P	10.00
	5	Obch	C		T	2	4	E	P	10.00
	6	OBC 1	C	M		2				4.00
OBC		**29**	**5**	**3**	**5**	**12**	**12**	**5**	**5**	**8.80**
S Delhi		**83**	**15**	**15**	**15**	**38**	**38**	**16**	**13**	**7.97**
	1	Gch 4	C	M	T	3	3	E	P	10.00
	2	Gch 2	C	M	T	2	2	E		10.00
	3	Gch 1	C	M	T	3	3	E	P	10.00
	4	Gch 1	C	M	T	2	2	E	P	10.00
	5	Gch 1	C	M	T	1	1	E	P	10.00
	6	Gch 3	C	M	T	2	2	E	P	10.00
	7	Gch 1	C		T	5	5	E		7.00
	8	Gcl 2	C	M	T	4	4	E		8.00
	9	Gcl 1	C	M	T	4	4	E		8.00

(Contd...)

(Contd...)

Sl.		Category-wise Literates Matric and Above	Communication: Cable/Sat. TV Weight 1	Communication: Mob. Weight 1	Communication: Tele. Weight 1	User: Comp-familiar Weight 2	User: Email/Transaction Weight 2	Content: Entertainment/info Weight 1	PC Weight 2	Score on 10 point Scale
	10	Gcl 1	C		T	4	4	E		8.00
	11	Gcl 1	C	M	T	6	6	E		8.00
	12	Gcl 2	C		T	6	6	E		8.00
GC		**56**	**12**	**10**	**12**	**42**	**42**	**12**	**5**	**8.90**
	1	Sch 2	C	M	T		2	E		6.00
	2	Scm 3		M				E	P	4.00
	3	Scm 3	C	M	T		2	E	P	8.00
	4	Scm 0	C	M	T	2	1	E		8.00
	5	Scl 0	C	M	T			E		4.00
	6	Scl 1	C	M	T	2	2	E		8.00
	7	Scl 1	C		T	1		E		5.00
	8	Scl 1	C		T			E		3.00
	9	Scl 2	C		T	2		E	p	7.00
	10	Scl 0		M						1.00
SC		**63**	**8**	**7**	**8**	**7**	**7**	**9**	**3**	**5.40**
	1	Obch 0	C	M	T			Y		4.00

(Contd...)

(Contd...)

Sl.		Category-wise Literates Matric and Above	Communication			User		Content		Score on 10 point Scale
			Cable/Sat. TV Weight 1	Mob. Weight 1	Tele. Weight 1	Comp-familiar Weight 2	Email/Transaction Weight 2	Entertainment/info Weight 1	PC Weight 2	
	2	Obcm 2	C		T			Y		3.00
	3	Obcl 2	C	M	T		1	Y	p	8.00
	4	Obcl 1	C	M	T	1	2	Y		8.00
	5	Obc 2	C		T	2		Y		5.00
	6	Obcl 2	C		T			Y		3.00
OBC		**34**	**5**	**5**	**5**	**3**	**4**	**5**	**1**	**5.20**
Punjabi Basti		**153**	**25**	**22**	**25**	**52**	**41**	**26**	**9**	**6.50**
Urban		**236**	**40**	**37**	**40**	**90**	**91**	**41**	**22**	**7.24**
	1	Gch 2	C		T	1		E	p	6.00
	2	Gcl 2				1		E		3.00
	3	Gcl 1	C		T		1	E		4.00
	4	Gcl 2	C		T	1	1	E		7.00
	5	Gcl 3	C	M	T	3		E	p	8.00
	6	Gcl 2		M			1	E		4.00
	7	Gcl 0					3	E	P	5.00

(Contd...)

(Contd...)

Sl.		*Category-wise Literates Matric and Above*	*Communication*			*User*		*Content*	*PC*	*Score on 10 point Scale*
			Cable/Sat. TV Weight 1	*Mob. Weight 1*	*Tele. Weight 1*	*Comp-familiar Weight 2*	*Email/Transaction Weight 2*	*Entertainment/info Weight 1*	*Weight 2*	
	8	Gcl 0	C		T			E		3.00
	9	Gcl 0	C		T			E		3.00
	10	Gcl 0						E		1.00
	11	Gcl 1		M				E		2.00
	12	Gcl 1	C	M	T			E		4.00
	13	Gcl 1	C	M	T	1	1	E		7.00
	14	Gcl 1	C	M	T	3	3	E	p	10.00
	15	Gcl 1	C					E		2.00
	16	Gcl 5	C		T	1	1	E		5.00
	17	Gcl 1	C		T			E		6.00
	18	Gcl 1	C		T			E		3.00
GC		**112**	**11**	**7**	**11**	**11**	**11**	**18**	**4**	**4.60**
	1	Sch 1	C		T			E		3.00
	2	Scm 1	C	M	T	2	2	E		8.00
	3	Scm 1	C	M	T	2	2	E	P	9.00

(Contd...)

(Contd...)

Sl.	Category-wise Literates Matric and Above	Communication: Cable/Sat. TV Weight 1	Communication: Mob. Weight 1	Communication: Tele. Weight 1	User: Comp-familiar Weight 2	User: Email/Transaction Weight 2	Content Entertainment/info Weight 1	PC Weight 2	Score on 10 point Scale
4	Scl 1	C	M	T	2	2	E		6.00
5	Scl 1	C	M	T			E		4.00
6	Scl 1	C	M	T			E		3.00
7	Scl 4		M			2			3.00
8	Scl 1	C	M	T			E		4.00
9	Scl 1	C	M	T			E		4.00
10	Scl 2		M				E		2.00
11	Scl 1	C	M	T	2	1	E		8.00
12	Scl 1	C	M	T	1		E		6.00
13	Scl 2						E		1.00
14	Scl 0		Y				E		2.00
SC	80	10	10	10	9	9	14	1	4.40
1	Obch 12	C	M	T		1	E	P	7.00
2	Obcm 3	C	M	T			E		4.00
3	Obcm 2	C	M	T			E		4.00
4	Obcm 1	C	M	T			E		4.00

(Contd...)

(Contd...)

Sl.	Category-wise Literates Matric and Above	Communication: Cable/Sat. TV Weight 1	Communication: Mob. Weight 1	Communication: Tele. Weight 1	User: Comp-familiar Weight 2	User: Email/Transaction Weight 2	Content Entertainment/info Weight 1	PC Weight 2	Score on 10 point Scale
5	Obcm 1	C	M	T			E		4.00
6	Obcm 3	C	M	T			E		4.00
7	Obcm 1	C		T	1	2	E	P	6.00
8	Obcm 1	C		T			E		3.00
9	Obcm 1	C	M	T			E		4.00
10	Obcm 2	C	M	T			E		4.00
11	Obcm 1	C	M	T			E		4.00
12	Obcm 2	C	M	T			E		4.00
13	Obcm 1	C		T	2		E		4.00
14	Obcm 1	C	M	T			E		4.00
15	Obcl 3	C	M	T			E		4.00
16	Obcl 1	C	M	T			E		4.00
17	Obcl 1	C	M	T			E		4.00
18	Obcl 1	C	M	T			E		4.00
19	Obcl 3	C	M	T			E		4.00
20	Obcl 1	C	M	T			E		4.00

(Contd...)

(Contd...)

Sl.	Category-wise Literates Matric and Above	Communication: Cable/Sat. TV Weight 1	Communication: Mob. Weight 1	Communication: Tele. Weight 1	User: Comp-familiar Weight 2	User: Email/Tran-saction Weight 2	Content Entertain-ment/info Weight 1	PC Weight 2	Score on 10 point Scale
21	Obcl 1	C	M	T			E		4.00
22	Obcl 1	C	M	T			E		4.00
23	Obcl 2	C		T			E		3.00
OBC	**142**	**23**	**21**	**23**	**2**	**2**	**24**	**2**	**4.20**
Mukund Pur	**334**	**31**	**38**	**31**	**22**	**22**	**56**	**7**	**5.00**
Grand Total	**570**	**71**	**75**	**71**	**113**	**113**	**97**	**29**	**6.12**

Note: The Ten point scale is based on a weight of 1 each for positive communication and content reply, 2 each for others: User and PC. Higher the score more is the family/strata conducive to digital/IT shift. The weight is calculated irrespective of quantity of response. For example, for numbers indicating internet and computer users could be counted as 2, their weights, no the numbers of users.

Also the additions vertically show total numbers, and horizontal additions of the weights give the score. The category wise and grand total scores are simple averages of the individual scores.

Gch: General category high income, GCM: General Category Middle Income, GLM: General category low income. Similarly, SC(Scheduled Caste and OBC(Other Backward Castes) have been assigned their income groups by suffixing H, M, and L, indicating high, middle, and low income groups as per the incomes defined: Middle Income: Above Rs.2.00 lakhs, Middle Income: between Rs. i.0 laks to Rs. 2.00laks ; and Low Income: Up to Rs.1.00 lakh.

Annexure 3: Computer Priority in Various Socio-Economic Strata/Families

Sl	Social and Economic Strata	Computer in One's Priority				
		TV 1	Car 2	Mobike 3	Mobile 4	PC 5
1	GCH6	Y	Y	0	Y	Y
2	GCh 4	Y	Y	Y	Y	Y
3	GCh 4	Y	Y	0	Y	Y
4	GCh 3	Y	0	0	Y	Y
5	GCh 5	Y	0	0	Y	Y
6	GCh 6	Y	0	Y	Y	Y
7	GCh 6	Y	Y	Y	Y	Y
8	GCl 8	Y	0	0	Y	0
9	GCl 2	Y	0	0	Y	0
10	GCl 2	Y	0	0	Y	0
GC	**46**	**9**	**4**	**3**	**10**	**7**
1	Sch 4	Y	0	0	Y	Y
2	Sch 4	Y	0	Y	Y	
SC	**8**	**2**	**0**	**1**	**2**	**1**
1	OBCh 4	Y	Y	Y		Y
2	OBCh 11	Y	Y	Y	Y	Y
3	OBCh 4	Y	Y	0	Y	Y

(Contd...)

Sl	Social and Economic Strata	Computer in One's Priority				
		TV 1	Car 2	Mobike 3	Mobile 4	PC 5
4	OBCh 6	Y	Y	0	Y	Y
5	OBCh4	Y	0	0		Y
6	OBCL	Y			Y	
OBC	**29**	**5**	**4**	**2**	**3**	**5**
S Delhi	**83**	**16**	**8**	**6**	**15**	**13**
1	Gch4	Y	0	0	Y	0
2	Gch6	Y	Y	Y	Y	Y
3	Gch7	Y	0	0	Y	Y
4	Gch6	Y	0	0	Y	Y
5	Gch4	Y	Y	Y	Y	Y
6	Gch2	Y	Y	0	Y	Y
7	Gch 3	Y	0	0	Y	0
8	Gcl 4	Y	0	0		0
9	Gcl4	Y	0	0	Y	0
10	Gcl4	Y	0	0	Y	0
11	Gcl6	Y	0	Y	Y	0

(Contd...)

(Contd...)

Sl	Social and Economic Strata	Computer in One's Priority				
		TV 1	Car 2	Mobike 3	Mobile 4	PC 5
12	Gcl6	Y	**0**	**3**	**10**	0
GC	**56**	**12**	**3**	Y	Y	**5**
1	Sch 11	Y	0	Y	Y	0
2	Scm 6	Y	0	0	Y	Y
3	Scm 8	Y	0	0	Y	Y
4	Scm 5	Y	0	0	Y	0
5	Scl 6	Y	0	0	Y	
6	Scl 6		0	Y	Y	0
7	Scl 7	Y	0	0	0	0
8	Scl 6	Y	0	0	0	0
9	Scl 3	Y	0	0	0	Y
10	Scl 5		0	0	0	0
SC	**63**	**8**	**0**	**3**	**7**	**3**
1	Obch 5	0	0	0	Y	0
2	Obcm 5	Y	0	0	Y	0
3	Obcl 5	Y	0	0	Y	Y

(Contd...)

(Contd...)

Sl	Social and Economic Strata	Computer in One's Priority				
		TV 1	*Car* 2	*Mobike* 3	*Mobile* 4	*PC* 5
4	Obcl 6	Y	0	0		0
5	Obcl 5	Y	0	0	Y	0
6	Obcl 8	Y	0	0	Y	0
OBC	**34**	**5**	**0**	**00**	**5**	**1**
P. Basti	**153**	**25**	**3**	**6**	**22**	**9**
Urban	**236**	**41**	**11**	**12**	**37**	**22**
1	Gch 5	Y	Y	Y	Y	Y
2	Gcl 7		0	0	Y	0
3	Gcl 5		0	0		0
4	Gcl 6		0	0		0
5	Gcl4		0	0	Y	Y
6	Gcl 4	Y	0	0	Y	0
7	Gcl 6	Y	0	0		Y
8	Gcl 4	Y	0	0		0
9	Gcl5	Y	0	0		0
10	Gcl5	Y	0	0		0

(Contd...)

(Contd...)

Sl	*Social and Economic Strata*	*Computer in One's Priority*				
		TV 1	*Car* 2	*Mobike* 3	*Mobile* 4	*PC* 5
11	Gck 5	Y	0	0		0
12	Gcl 9	Y	0	0		0
13	Gcl 6	Y	0	Y	Y	0
14	Gcl 7	Y	0	0	Y	Y
15	Gcl 6	0	0	0		0
16	Gcl 5	0	0	0	Y	0
17	Gcl 8	**0**	**0**	**0**		0
18	1gcl 5	0	0	0		0
GC	**112**	**10**	0	**20**	**7**	**4**
1	Sch 6	Y	0	Y		0
2	Scm 6	Y	0	Y	Y	0
3	Scm 5	Y	0	Y	Y	Y
4	Scl 7	Y	0	Y	Y	0
5	Scl 6	Y	0	Y	Y	0
6	Scl	Y	0	Y	Y	0

(Contd...)

(Contd...)

Sl	Social and Economic Strata	Computer in One's Priority				
		TV 1	Car 2	Mobike 3	Mobile 4	PC 5
7	Scl 5	Y	0	Y	Y	0
8	7scl	Y	0	Y	Y	0
9	Scl 4	0	0	Y	Y	0
10	Scl 7	Y	0	Y		0
11	Scl 5	Y	0	Y	Y	0
12	Scl 6	Y	0	0	Y	0
13	Scl 7	0	0	Y	0	0
14	Scl 6	0	0	Y	0	0
SC	**80**	**11**	**0**	**11**	**10**	**1**
1	Obch1 7	Y	Y	Y	Y	Y
2	Obcm 8	Y	0	0	Y	0
3	Obcm 5	Y	0	Y	Y	0
4	Obcm 5	Y	0	0	Y	0
5	Obcm 7	Y	0	0	Y	0
6	Obcm 5	Y	0	Y	Y	0
7	Obcm 6	Y	0	0	Y	Y
8	Obcm 4	Y	0	0	Y	0

(Contd...)

(Contd...)

Sl	Social and Economic Strata	Computer in One's Priority				
		TV 1	*Car* 2	*Mobike* 3	*Mobile* 4	*PC* 5
9	Obcm 7	Y	0	Y	Y	0
10	Obcm 7	Y	0	Y	Y	0
11	Obcm 7	Y	0	0	Y	0
12	Obcm 4	Y	0	0	Y	0
13	Obcm 8	Y	0	0		0
14	Obcm 8	Y	0	0	Y	0
15	Obcl 7		0	0	Y	0
16	Obcl 4	Y	0	Y	Y	0
17	Obcl 6	Y	0	0	Y	0
18	Obcl 6	Y	0	0	Y	0
19	Obcl 8	Y	0	0	Y	0
20	Obcl 5	Y	0	0	Y	0
21	Obcl 5		0	0	Y	0
22	Obcl 6	Y	0	0	Y	0
23	Obcl 3	Y	0	0		0
OBC	**142**	**21**	**1**	**6**	**21**	**2**
Mukund Pur	**334**	**42**	**9**	**19**	**38**	**7**
Grand Total	**570**	**83**	**20**	**30**	**75**	**29**

Note: The Y's in the columns pertaining to each entry indicate availability/positive answer of the item.

Annexure 4 : Master Table 1: Space and Category-wise Literacy, Occupation, Income

Sl No.	*GC/SC/OBC (Members)*	*Education*			*Occupation*			*Income (Rs.)*			*Remarks*
		M/TPT	*UG/G*	*PG*	*IT*	*NIT*	*Farm*	*HI*	*MI*	*LI*	
1	*2*	*3*	*4*	*5*	*6*	*7*	*8*	*9*	*10*	*11*	
1	GCh 6	4	1/1		...	Business	... .	400000	...	...	
2	Gch 4	1	1/1			Dancer		350000			
3	Gch 4	1	1/2			Gov		345000			
4	Gch 3	2	1 G	1		Shop		341000			
5	Gch 5		3/2			Gov.		335000			
6	Gch 6	1	1 g			Gov.		333000			
7	Gcm 6	1	3 g	2		Gov.			200000		
8	Gcl 8	1				Drv.				25000	
9	Gcl 2	1				Au drv.				24000	
10	Gcl 2	2				Farmwk.				25000	
Total	**46**	**14**	**17**	**3**	**0**	**10**		**6**	**1**	**3**	
1	Sch 4		1/2			Gov.		3000000			
2	Schl 4	2	1 g			Pvt. job				40000	
Total	**8**	**2**	**4**	**0**	**0**	**2**		**1**	**1**		
1	Obch 4		1 g			Bsn.		300000			
2	Obch 11	1	6 g			Bsn.		300000			

(Contd...)

(Contd...)

Sl No.	GC/SC/OBC (Members)	Education			Occupation			Income (Rs.)			Remarks
		M/TPT	UG/G	PG	IT	NIT	Farm	HI	MI	LI	
1	2	3	4	5	6	7	8	9	10	11	
3	Obch 4	1	G2			Bsn.		250000			
4	Obch 6	1/1	1/2			Bsn		260000			
5	Obch 4					Art		125000		18000	
6	OBC 1										
Total	**29**	**4**	**12**	**0**	**0**	**5**		**4**		**1**	
South Delh (18)	**83**	**20**	**33**	**3**	**0**	**17**		**12**		**5**	
1	Gch 4	3	1 g		Mgr. IT			500000			
2	6	2				Bsn.		250000			
3	7	1		1		Rtd.		230000			
4	6	1			Mob. shop				180000		
5	4	1				Bsn.		200000			
6	2	1	1			Teach.			130000		
7	Gch 3	3				Bsn.			125000		
8	Gcl 4	1				Taxi dvr.				60000	

(Contd...)

(Contd...)

Sl No.	GC/SC/OBC (Members)	Education			Occupation			Income (Rs.)			Remarks
		M/TPT	UG/G	PG	IT	NIT	Farm	HI	MI	LI	
1	2	3	4	5	6	7	8	9	10	11	
9	Gcl 4	1	1 g		Video					50000	
10	Gcl 4	1				Teach.				36000	
11	Gcl 6		1 g			Bsn.				35000	
12	Gcl 6	1			Shop					32000	
Total	**56**	**15**	**3**	**3**	**3**	**9**		**4**	**3**	**5**	
1	Sch 11	3				Bsn.		200000			
2	Scm 6	2				Bsn.			130000		
3	Scm 8	1	2		Comp. opr				135000		
4	Scm 5	1	2			Gov.			120000		
5	Scl 6					Drv.				60000	
6	Scl 6					Tailor				50000	
7	Scl 7	1				Job pvt.				45000	
8	Scl 6	1				Pvt job				36000	
9	Scl 3	1				Bsn.				18000	

(Contd...)

(Contd...)

Sl No.	*GC/SC/OBC (Members)*	*Education*			*Occupation*			*Income (Rs.)*			*Remarks*
		M/TPT	*UG/G*	*PG*	*IT*	*NIT*	*Farm*	*HI*	*MI*	*LI*	
1	*2*	*3*	*4*	*5*	*6*	*7*	*8*	*9*	*10*	*11*	
10	Scl5	2				Gardener				20000	
Total	**63**	**12**	**2**		**1**	**9**		**1**	**3**	**7**	
1	Obch 5					Shop		250000			
2	Obcm 5	1	1			Gov.			190000		
3	Obcl 5	1	1			Gov.			125000		
4	Obcl 6	1				Gov.			115000		
5	Obcl 5	2				Bsn				60000	
6	Obcl 8	1	1			Account				36000	
Total	**34**	**6**	**3**	**3**		**6**		**1**	**3**	**2**	
P B(28)	**153**	**33**	**8**	**6**	**4**	**23**		**5**	**9**	**12**	
Urban(45)		**236**	**53**	**41**	**9**	**21**	**40**		**17**	**21**	**17**
1	Gch 5	1	1		Bsn.			300000			
2	Gcl 7	1	1		Shop				125000		
3	Gcm 5	1			Gov.				140000		
4	Gcl 6	1	1		Au. drv.					60000	

(Contd...)

(Contd...)

Sl No.	GC/SC/OBC (Members)	Education			Occupation			Income (Rs.)			Remarks
		M/TPT	UG/G	PG	IT	NIT	Farm	HI	MI	LI	
1	2	3	4	5	6	7	8	9	10	11	
5	Gcm4	1	2		Pvt Job					60000	
6	Gcl 4	2			Tailor					50000	
7	Gcl 6						Fl			50000	
8	Gcl 4				Shop					50000	
9	5						F			40000	
10	5						F			40000	
11	5	1			R		Fl			36000	
12	9	1	½		Carpenter					30000	
13	6	1	1		Shop					25000	
14	7	1	2		Job					60000	
15	6	1					F 1			36000	
16	5	5					F 1			36000	
17	8	1					F 1			36000	
18	15	1			Bsn.					34000	
Total	**112**	**19**	**11**		**13**		**7**	**1**	**2**	**15**	

(Contd...)

(Contd...)

Sl No.	GC/SC/OBC (Members)	Education			Occupation			Income (Rs.)			Remarks
		M/TPT	UG/G	PG	IT	NIT	Farm	HI	MI	LI	
1	2	3	4	5	6	7	8	9	10	11	
1	Sch 6	1	1			Bsn.		210000			
2	Sch 6	1	2			Bsn.			130000		
3	Scm 5	1				Job			125000		
4	Scl 7	1	1			Shop			110000		
5	Scl 6	1				Drv.				60000	
6	Scl 3	1					F 1			45000	
7	Scl 5	4				Bsn.				50000	
8	Scl 7	1	1			Waiter				40000	
9	Scl 4	1					F 1			35000	
10	Scl 7	2					F 1			36000	
11	Scl 5	1				Job				38000	
12	Scl 6	1				Garment				45000	
13	Scl 7	2					F 1			37000	
14	Scl 6						Fl			35000	
Total	**80**	**18**	**5**		**0**	**9**	**5**	**1**	**5**	**10**	

(Contd...)

(Contd...)

Sl No.	GC/SC/OBC (Members)	Education			Occupation			Income (Rs.)			Remarks
		M/TPT	UG/G	PG	IT	NIT	Farm	HI	MI	LI	
1	2	3	4	5	6	7	8	9	10	11	
1	Obch17	6	6	5			Farm	300000			
2	Obcm8	3	2		Comp				120000		
3	Obcm5	2				Teacher			110000		
4	Obcm5	1				Gov.			120000		
5	Obcm7	1				Gov.			130000		
6	Obcm5	3				Au. drv.				95000	
7	Obcm6	1				Supervis.				70000	
8	Obcm4	1	1			Job				70000	
9	Obcm7	1	2			Bsn.				40000	
10	Obcm7	2				Mech.				65000	
11	Obcm7	1				Estate				60000	
12	Obcm4	2	1			Garden				50000	
13	Obcm 8	1	1				Farmer			50000	
14	Obcm 8	1	1				Farmer			50000	
15	Obcl 7	3	1							30000	

(Contd...)

(Contd...)

Sl No.	*GC/SC/OBC (Members)*	*Education*			*Occupation*			*Income (Rs.)*			*Remarks*
		M/TPT	*UG/G*	*PG*	*IT*	*NIT*	*Farm*	*HI*	*MI*	*LI*	
1	*2*	*3*	*4*	*5*	*6*	*7*	*8*	*9*	*10*	*11*	
16	Obcl 4	1								30000	
17	Obcl 6	1								50000	
18	Obcl 6	1	1				Farmer			50000	
19	Obcl 8	4				Job				45000	
20	Obcl 5	1	1				FL			49000	
21	Obcl 5	1	1		Comp					45000	
22	Obcl 6	1								45000	
23	Obcl 3	2								45000	
Total	**142**	**43**	**18**	**5**	**2**	**11**	**5**	**1**	**4**	**20**	
MPr(56)	**334**	**80**	**34**	**5**	**13**	**20**	**17**	**3**	**11**	**35**	
Grand Total(102)	**570**	**133**	**75**	**14**	**47**	**60**	**17**	**20**	**32**	**52**	

Annexure 5: Master Table 2: Space and Category-wise Family Heads

Sl No.	GC/SC/OBC (Member)	House			Family Overheads			
		Palatial	Good	Shanty	TV	Car	Mobike	Mobile
1	2	3	4		5	6	7	8
1	GCH 6	p			y	Y…		y..
2	Gch 4		g		Y	Y	Y	Y
3	Gch 4		G		Y	Y		Y
4	Gch 3		G		Y			Y
5	Gch 5	P			Y			Y
6	Gch 6		G		Y		Y	Y
7	Gch 6		G		Y	Y	Y	Y
8	Gcl 8			S	Y			Y
9	Gcl 2			S	Y			Y
10	Gcl 2			S	Y			Y
Total	**46**	**2**	**5**	**3**	**9**	**4**	**3**	**10**
1	Sch 4		y		Y			Y
2	Sch 4		y		Y		y	Y
Total	**8**		**2**		**2**		**1**	**2**
1	Obch 4		G		Y	y	Y	
2	Obch 11		G		Y	Y	Y	Y

(Contd...)

(Contd...)

Sl No.	*GC/SC/OBC (Member)*	*House*			*Family Overheads*			
		Palatial	*Good*	*Shanty*	*TV*	*Car*	*Mobike*	*Mobile*
1	*2*	*3*	*4*		*5*	*6*	*7*	*8*
3	Obch 4		G		Y	y		Y
4	Obch6		G		Y	y		Y
5	Obch4		G		Y			
6	OBCl			S				M
Total	**29**	**0**	**5**		**5**	**4**	**2**	**3**
South Delhi	**83**	**2**	**12**	**3**	**16**	**8**	**6**	**15**
1	Gch4	p			Y			Y
2	6				Y			Y
3	7		G		Y	y	Y	Y
4	6		G		Y			Y
5	4	P			Y			Y
6	2		G		Y	Y	Y	Y
7	Gch 3			S	Y	y		Y
8	Gcl 4			S	Y			
9	4			S	Y			Y
10	4			S	Y			Y

(Contd...)

(Contd...)

Sl No.	GC/SC/OBC (Member)	House			Family Overheads			
		Palatial	Good	Shanty	TV	Car	Mobike	Mobile
1	2	3	4		5	6	7	8
11				S	Y			
12				S	Y		Y	Y
Total	**56**	**2**	**3**	**7**	**12**	**3**	**3**	**10**
1	Sch 11		G		Y		Y	Y
2	Scm 6		G		Y		Y	Y
3	Scm 8				Y			Y
4	Scm 5		G		Y			Y
5	Scl 6			s	Y			Y
6	Scl 6							Y
7	Scl 7			S	Y		Y	Y
8	Scl 6			S	Y			
9	Scl 3		G	S	Y			
Total	**56**	**0**	**6**	**4**	**8**	**0**	**3**	**7**
1	Obch 5	p						Y
2	Obcm 5			S	Y			Y
3	Obcl 5			S	Y			Y
4	Obcl 6			S	Y			

(Contd...)

(Contd...)

Sl No.	GC/SC/OBC (Member)	House			Family Overheads			
		Palatial	Good	Shanty	TV	Car	Mobike	Mobile
1	2	3	4		5	6	7	8
5	Obcl 5			S	Y			Y
6	Obcl 8			S	Y			Y
Total	**34**	**1**	**9**	**5**	**5**	**0**	**0**	**5**
P B	**153**	**3**	**18**	**16**	**25**	**3**	**6**	**22**
Urban	**236**	**5**	**30**	**19**	**41**	**11**	**12**	**37**
1	Gch 5		G		Y	Y	Y	Y
2	Gcl 7		G					Y
3	Gcl 5		G					
4	Gcl 6		G					
5	Gcl4			S				
6	Gcl 4		G					
7	Gcl 6		G					Y
8	Gcl 4			S	Y			Y
9	5		G		Y			
10	5			S	Y			
11	5		G		Y			

(Contd...)

(Contd...)

Sl No.	GC/SC/OBC (Member)	House			Family Overheads			
		Palatial	Good	Shanty	TV	Car	Mobike	Mobile
1	2	3	4		5	6	7	8
12	9			S	Y			
13	6			S	Y			Y
14	7		G		Y			Y
15	6		G		Y		Y	
16	5				Y			Y
17	8							
18	15							
Total	**112**		**10**	**5**	**10**		**2**	**7**
1	Sch 6	Y	G	Bsn	Y		Y	
2	Scm 6	Y	G		Y		Y	
3	Scm 5		G		Y		Y	
4	Scl 7		G		Y		Y	L
5	Scl 6			S	Y		Y	L
6	Scl		G		Y		Y	L
7	5		G		Y		Y	L
8	7		G		Y		Y	L

(Contd...)

(Contd...)

Sl No.	*GC/SC/OBC (Member)*	*House*			*Family Overheads*			
		Palatial	*Good*	*Shanty*	*TV*	*Car*	*Mobike*	*Mobile*
1	*2*	*3*	*4*		*5*	*6*	*7*	*8*
9	4		G				Y	L
10	7			S	Y		Y	L
11	5			S	Y		Y	L
12	6		G		Y			
13	7			S			Y	L
14	6	2		S			Y	L
Total	**80**	**2**	**8**	**5**	**11**	**0**	**11**	**10**
1	Obch 17				Y	Y	Y	Y
2	Obcm 8				Y			Y
3	Obcm 5		G		Y		Y	Y
4	Obcm 5		G		Y			Y
5	Obcm 7		G		Y			Y
6	Obcm 5		G		Y			Y
7	Obcm 6			S	Y			Y
8	Obcm 4		G		Y		Y	Y
9	Obcm 7		G		Y			

(Contd...)

(Contd...)

Sl No.	GC/SC/OBC (Member)	House			Family Overheads			
		Palatial	Good	Shanty	TV	Car	Mobike	Mobile
1	2	3	4		5	6	7	8
10	Obcm 7		G		Y			
11	Obcm 7		G		Y		Y	Y
12	Obcm 4		G		Y		Y	Y
13	Obcm 8		G		Y			Y
14	Obcm 8			S	Y			Y
15	Obcl 7		G					
16	Obcl 4		G		Y			Y
17	Obcl 6		G		Y			Y
18	Obcl 6		G		Y		Y	Y
19								
Obcl 8			**S**	**Y**			**Y**	
20	Obcl 5			S	Y			Y
21	Obcl 5			S				Y
22	Obcl 6			S	Y			Y
23	Obcl 3			S	Y			Y
Total	**142**	**0**	**14**	**8**	**21**	**1**	**6**	**21**
Mukund Pur	**334**	**0**	**32**	**23**	**42**	**9**	**19**	**38**
Grand Total	**570**	**5**	**60**	**43**	**83**	**20**	**30**	**75**

Annexure 6 : Master Table 3: Category/Area-wise Infostructure Status

Sl	*GC/SC/OBC*	*Computing Facilities*			*Communication Facilities*			*Content*		
No.	*(Member)*	*PC*	*Mobs.*	*Digitcam*	*Telephony*	*Cable*	*Satellite*	*Entertainment*	*Publishing*	*Info.*
1	*2*	*3*	*4*	*5*	*6*	*7*	*8*	*9*	*10*	*11*
1	GCH 6	Y	Y	Y	Y	Y		Y		Y
2	Gch 4	Y	Y		Y	Y		Y		Y
3	Gch 4	Y	Y		Y	Y		Y		Y
4	Gch 3	Y	Y		Y	Y		Y		Y
5	Gch 5	Y	Y		Y	Y		Y		
6	Gch 6	Y	Y		Y	Y		Y		
7	Gch 6	Y	Y		Y	Y		Y		Y
8	Gcl 8		Y		Y	Y		Y		Y
9	Gcl 2		Y		Y	Y		Y		
10	Gcl 2		Y		Y	Y		Y		
Total	**46**	**7**	**10**		**10**	**10**		**10**		**6**
1	Sch 4	Y	Y		Y	Y				
2	Sch 4					Y		Y		Y
Total	**8**	**1**	**1**	**0**	**1**	**2**		**1**		**1**
1	Obch 4	Y	Y	Y	Y	Y		Y		
2	Obch 11	Y	Y		Y	Y		Y		y
3	Obch 4	Y	Y	Y	Y	Y		Y		

(Contd...)

(Contd...)

Sl	*GC/SC/OBC*	*Computing Facilities*			*Communication Facilities*			*Content*		
No.	*(Member)*	*PC*	*Mobs.*	*Digitcam*	*Telephony*	*Cable*	*Satellite*	*Entertainment*	*Publishing*	*Info.*
1	*2*	*3*	*4*	*5*	*6*	*7*	*8*	*9*	*10*	*11*
4	Obch 6	Y	Y	Y	Y	Y		Y		Y
5	Obch 4	Y	Y	Y	Y	Y		Y		Y
6	OBC 1		Y					Y		Y
Total	**29**	**5**	**5**	**4**	**5**	**5**		**5**		**3**
South Delhi		**83**	**13**	**16**	**5**	**15**	**15**	**15**		
1	Gch 4	Y	Y		Y	Y		Y		Y
2	6				Y	Y		Y		Y
3	7	Y	Y		Y	Y		Y		Y
4	6	Y	Y		Y	Y		Y		Y
5	4	Y	Y		Y	Y		Y		Y
6	2	Y			Y	Y		Y		Y
7	Gch 3				Y	Y		Y		Y
8	Gcl 4			Y	Y	Y		Y		Y
9	4				Y	Y		Y		Y
10	4				Y	Y		Y		

(Contd...)

(Contd...)

Sl	*GC/SC/OBC*	*Computing Facilities*			*Communication Facilities*			*Content*		
No.	*(Member)*	*PC*	*Mobs.*	*Digitcam*	*Telephony*	*Cable*	*Satellite*	*Entertainment*	*Publishing*	*Info.*
1	*2*	*3*	*4*	*5*	*6*	*7*	*8*	*9*	*10*	*11*
11	6				Y	Y		Y		Y
12	6				Y	Y		Y		Y
Total	**56**	**5**	**4**	**1**	**12**	**11**	**1**	**12**		**11**
1	Sch 11				Y	Y		Y		Y
2	Scm 6	Y				Y		Y		Y
3	Scm 8	Y	Y		Y	Y		Y		
4	Scm 5				Y	Y		Y		Y
5	Scl 6				Y	Y		Y		Y
6	Scl 6				Y	Y		Y		
7	Scl 7		Y		Y	Y		Y		
8	Scl 6		Y		Y	Y		Y		Y
9	Scl 3	Y			Y	Y		Y		Y
10	Scl 5					Y				
Total	**63**	**3**	**3**	**0**	**8**	**9**	**1**	**9**		**6**
1	Obch 5				Y	Y		Y		Y
2	Obcm 5				Y	Y		Y		Y

(Contd...)

(Contd...)

Sl	GC/SC/OBC	Computing Facilities			Communication Facilities			Content		
No.	(Member)	PC	Mobs.	Digitcam	Telephony	Cable	Satellite	Entertainment	Publishing	Info.
1	2	3	4	5	6	7	8	9	10	11
3	Obcl5	Y			Y	Y		Y		Y
4	Obcl6				Y	Y		Y		Y
5	Obcl5				Y	Y		Y		Y
6	Obcl 8				Y	Y		Y		
Total	**34**	**1**	**1**		**5**	**5**		**5**		**5**
PB	**153**	**9**	**1**		**25**	**25**	**1**	**26**		**22**
Urban Area	**236**	**22**	**2**		**40**	**40**		**41**		**31**
1	Gch 5	Y			Y			Y		Y
2	Gcl 7							Y		Y
3	Gcl 5				Y			Y		Y
4	Gcl 6				Y			Y		Y
5	Gcl 4	Y			Y			Y		Y
6	Gcl 4							Y		Y
7	Gcl 6	Y				SAT		Y		Y
8	Gcl 4				Y			Y		Y

(Contd...)

(Contd...)

Sl	*GC/SC/OBC*	*Computing Facilities*			*Communication Facilities*			*Content*		
No.	*(Member)*	*PC*	*Mobs.*	*Digitcam*	*Telephony*	*Cable*	*Satellite*	*Entertainment*	*Publishing*	*Info.*
1	*2*	*3*	*4*	*5*	*6*	*7*	*8*	*9*	*10*	*11*
9	5				Y			Y		Y
10	5					SAT		Y		Y
11	5					SAT		Y		Y
12	9		Y		Y			Y		Y
13	6				Y			Y		Y
14	7	Y			Y			Y		Y
15	6					SAT		Y		Y
16	5				Y			Y		Y
17	8				Y			Y		Y
18	15				Y			Y		Y
Total	**112**	**4**	**1**		**11**	**4**	**15**	**18**		**18**
1	Sch 6				Y	Y		Y		Y
2	Scm 6				Y	Y		Y		Y
3	Scm 5	Y	Y		Y	Y		Y		Y
4	Scl 7				Y	Y		Y		Y

(Contd...)

(Contd...)

Sl	*GC/SC/OBC*	*Computing Facilities*			*Communication Facilities*			*Content*		
No.	*(Member)*	*PC*	*Mobs.*	*Digitcam*	*Telephony*	*Cable*	*Satellite*	*Entertainment*	*Publishing*	*Info.*
1	*2*	*3*	*4*	*5*	*6*	*7*	*8*	*9*	*10*	*11*
5	Scl 6				Y	Y		Y		Y
6	Scl		Y		Y	Y		Y		Y
7	5						SAT			Y
8	7		Y		Y	Y		Y		Y
9	4		Y		Y	Y		Y		Y
10	7						SAT	Y		Y
11	5				Y	Y		Y		Y
12	6				Y	Y		Y		Y
13	7							Y		Y
14	6							Y		Y
Total	**80**	**1**	**4**		**10**	**10**	**2**	**14**		**14**
1	Obch 17	Y			Y	Y		Y		Y
2	Obcm 8		Y		Y	Y		Y		Y
3	Obcm 5				Y	Y		Y		Y
4	Obcm 5				Y	Y		Y		Y

(Contd...)

(Contd...)

Sl	GC/SC/OBC	Computing Facilities			Communication Facilities			Content		
No.	(Member)	PC	Mobs.	Digitcam	Telephony	Cable	Satellite	Entertainment	Publishing	Info.
1	2	3	4	5	6	7	8	9	10	11
5	Obcm 7				Y	Y		Y		Y
6	Obcm 5				Y	Y		Y		Y
7	Obcm 6	Y			Y	Y		Y		Y
8	Obcm 4		Y		Y	Y		Y		Y
9	Obcm 7				Y	Y		Y		Y
10	Obcm 7				Y	Y		Y		Y
11	Obcm 7				Y	Y		YY		Y
12	Obcm 4		Y		Y	Y		Y		Y
13	Obcm 8		Y		Y	Y		Y		Y
14	Obcm 8		Y		Y	Y		Y		Y
15	Obcl 7		Y		Y	Y		Y		
16	Obcl 4				Y	Y		Y		Y
17	Obcl 6				YY	Y		Y		Y
18	Obcl 6		Y		Y	Y		Y		
19	Obcl 8				Y	Y		Y		

(Contd...)

(Contd...)

Sl No.	GC/SC/OBC (Member)	Computing Facilities			Communication Facilities			Content		
		PC	Mobs.	Digitcam	Telephony	Cable	Satellite	Entertainment	Publishing	Info.
1	2	3	4	5	6	7	8	9	10	11
20	Obcl 5		Y		Y	Y		Y		Y
21	Obcl 5		Y		Y	Y		Y		Y
22	Obcl 6		Y		Y	Y		Y		Y
23	Obcl 3		Y		Y	Y		Y		
24	Obcl 4		Y		Y	Y		Y		
Total	**142**	**2**	**12**		**23**	**24**		**24**		**14**
Mukund Pur	**334**	**7**	**17**		**31**	**38**		**56**		**46**
Grand Total	**570**	**29**	**19**		**71**	**78**		**97**		**77**

Annexure 7: Master Table 4: Category/Area-wise IT Awareness/Application

Sl No.	*GC/SC/OBC (Members)*	*Awareness/Application*			*Future Perception*			*Future Plans*			*Problems*
		Use	*Email*	*Trans-actions*	*Bright*	*Little Future*	*No future*	*Training/ Emp/*	*Suggestions/ Probs.*		
1	*2*	*3*	*4*	*5*	*6*	*7*	*8*	*9*		*10*	
1	GCH 6	3	2		Y			Emp.	ITS	..	
2	Gch 4	2	2			Y		Emp.	ITS		PTRn
3	Gch 4	3	2		Y			Emp.	CAT		
4	Gch 3	2	1		Y			Emp.	AffCom	P	
5	Gch 5	3			Y			Education	CAWaWo		PTRn
6	Gch 6	4	4		Y			Education	RCEdIn		
7	Gch 6	3				Y		Emp.	ITS		
8	Gcl 8				Y	Y		Emp.	ITS/ AffCom	P	PTRn
9	Gcl 2	1						Emp.	AffCom	P	
10	Gcl 2							Education	ITS /AffCom	P	
Total	**37**	**20**	**11**		**7**	**3**					
1	Sch 4	3	2		y		1	Emp.	ITS /AffCom	P	PTRn
2	Sch 4	2	2						AffCom		
Total	**8**	**5**	**4**		**1**		**1**	**Education**			
1	Obc h 4	3	1		Y			Education	ITS /AffCom	P	PTRn
2	Obch11	3	2		Y			Emp	ITS /AffCom	P	

(Contd...)

(Contd...)

Sl No.	GC/SC/OBC (Members)	Awareness/Application			Future Perception			Future Plans		Problems
		Use	Email	Trans-actions	Bright	Little Future	No future	Training/ Emp/	Suggestions/ Probs.	
1	2	3	4	5	6	7	8	9		10
3	Obch4	2	3		Y			Education	ITS /AffCom	P
4	Obch6	4				Y		Emp.	ITS /AffCom	P
5	Obch4							Emp.	ITS /AffCom	P
6	OBCl									
Total	**26**	**12**	**6**		**4**	**1**	**1**			
South Delhi		**38**	**21**		**12**	**4**	**1**			
1	Gch4	3	3	1	Y			IT trainning	AWS/ ITS	
2	6	2	1	1	Y				ITS /LP	
3	7	3	1		Y				ITS /LPS	
4	6	2	2	1	Y				AWS/ ITS	Poor recp.
5	4	1	1	1	Y				ITS	
6	2	2	2		Y					
7	Gch 3	5			Y			Comp. training	AWS/ ITS/ LP	
8	Gcl 4	4			Y				RCEd	Poor recp.
9	4	4			Y				AWS/ ITS	RCEdIn

(Contd...)

(Contd...)

Sl No.	*GC/SC/OBC (Members)*	*Awareness/Application*			*Future Perception*				*Future Plans*	*Problems*
		Use	*Email*	*Trans-actions*	*Bright*	*Little Future*	*No future*	*Training/ Emp/*	*Suggestions/ Probs.*	
1	*2*	*3*	*4*	*5*	*6*	*7*	*8*	*9*		*10*
10	4	4			Y		Y		ITS	
11	6	6			Y				LP	
12	6	6			Y				LP	
Total	**52**	**42**	**10**	**4**	**11**		**1**			**Poor recp**
1	Sch11	2	2		Y				ITS/ LP	
2	Scm 6				Y				RCEd	
3	Scm 8	2	2		Y				RCE	
4	Scm 5	1	1		Y				LP	
5	Scl 6				Y				ITS/ LP	
6	Scl 6	2	2		Y				ITS/ LP	
7	Scl 7						y		ITS/ LP	
8	Scl 6					Y			LP	Poor recp
9	Scl 3								LP	
Total	**58**	**7**	**7**		**7**	**1**	**1**			
1	Obch 5				Y				RCEdIn	

(Contd...)

(Contd...)

Sl No.	GC/SC/OBC (Members)	Awareness/Application			Future Perception			Future Plans		Problems
		Use	Email	Trans-actions	Bright	Little Future	No future	Training/ Emp/	Suggestions/ Probs.	
1	2	3	4	5	6	7	8	9	10	
2	Obcm 5	1	1		Y				ITS/ AffCom	P
3	Obcl5	2	1		Y				ITS/ L P	
4	Obcl6				Y				ITS/ LP	
5	Obcl5				Y				ITS/ L AWS	
6	Obcl 8		1				Y		ITS	
Total	**34**	**4**	**3**		**5**					
P B	**28**	**41**			**24**	**1**	**1**			
Urban	**45**	**91**	**83**		**36**	**5**	**1**			
1	Gch 5	1	1		Y			Ermp.	ITS/ AffCom	P
2	Gcl 7	1	1		Y			Ermp.	RCEdIn	
3	Gcl 5					Y		Ermp.	AffCom P / ITS	
4	Gcl 6	1	1					Ermp.	CAWaWo/ ITS	
5	Gcl 4	3	2		Y				AffCom P	
6	Gcl 4				Y			Ermp.	ITS in village/	
7	Gcl 6							Ermp.	RCEdIn	

(Contd...)

(Contd...)

Sl No.	GC/SC/OBC (Members)	*Awareness/Application* Use	Email	Trans-actions	*Future Perception* Bright	Little Future	No future	*Future Plans* Training/ Emp/	Suggestions/ Probs.	*Problems*
1	2	3	4	5	6	7	8	9	10	
8	Gcl 4				Y			Education	ITS/ AffCom	
9	5				Y			Ermp.	AffCom laon	
10	5							Ermp.	RCEdIn	
11	5					Y		Ermp.	RCEdIn	
12	9				Y			Education	Comp loans	
13	6	1	1					Ermp.	ITS/ AffCom P	
14	7	3	1					Ermp.	ITS/ AffCom P	
15	6				Y			Ermp.	ITS/ AffCom P	
16	5	1	1		Y			IT education		CAWaWo
17	8							Ermp.	RCEdIn	
18	15					Y		Ermp.	CAWaWo/ ITS	
Total	**112**	**11**	**8**		**10**	**3**	**1**			
1	**2**									
1	Sch 6				Y			Education	RCEdIn	
2	Scm 6	2	1		Y			Education	ITS/ AffCom P	

(Contd...)

(Contd...)

Sl No.	GC/SC/OBC (Members)	Awareness/Application			Future Perception			Future Plans		Problems
		Use	Email	Trans-actions	Bright	Little Future	No future	Training/ Emp/	Suggestions/ Probs.	
1	2	3	4	5	6	7	8	9	10	
3	Scm 5	2	1			Y		Emp.	AffCom P / ITS	
4	Scl 7	2	1		Y			Ermp	CAWaWo/ ITS	
5	Scl 6				Y	Y		Ermp	AffCom P	
6	Scl				Y			Ermp	ITS in village/	
7	5	2	2		Y				RCEdIn	
8	7				Y	Y		Education	AffCom	
9	4				Y			Education	AffCom laon	
10	7				Y			Education	RCEdIn	
11	5	1	1		Y			Education	RCEdIn	
12	6				Y			Ermp	AffCom	
13	7				Y			Education		
14	6				Y			Education		
Total	**80**	**9**	**6**		**Y**	**3**	**1**			
1	Obch17	Y			Y	Y		Education	ITS	
2	Obcm8		Y		Y	Y		Education	ITS	

(Contd...)

(Contd...)

Sl No.	GC/SC/OBC (Members)	Awareness/Application			Future Perception			Future Plans		Problems
		Use	Email	Trans-actions	Bright	Little Future	No future	Training/ Emp/	Suggestions/ Probs.	
1	2	3	4	5	6	7	8	9		10
3	Obcm 5				Y	Y		Emp	CAT	
4	Obcm 5				Y	Y		Ermp	AffCom	P
5	Obcm 7				Y	Y		Ermp	CAWaWo	
6	Obcm 5				Y	Y		Ermp	RCEdIn	
7	Obcm 6	Y			Y	Y			ITS	
8	Obcm 4		Y		Y	Y		Education	ITS/ AffCom	P
9	Obcm 7				Y	Y		Education	AffCom	P
10	Obcm 7				Y	Y		Education	ITS /AffCom	P
11	Obcm 7				Y	Y		Education	ITS	
12	Obcm 4		Y		Y	Y		Ermp	ITS	
13	Obcm 8		Y		Y	Y		Education	CAT	
14	Obcm 8		Y		Y	Y		Education	AffCom	P
15	Obcl 7		Y		Y	Y		Education	CAWaWo	
16	Obcl 4				Y	Y		Education	RCEdIn	
17	Obcl 6				Y	Y		Emp	ITS	

(Contd...)

(Contd...)

Sl No.	*GC/SC/OBC (Members)*	*Awareness/Application*			*Future Perception*			*Future Plans*		*Problems*
		Use	*Email*	*Trans-actions*	*Bright*	*Little Future*	*No future*	*Training/ Emp/*	*Suggestions/ Probs.*	
1	*2*	*3*	*4*	*5*	*6*	*7*	*8*	*9*		*10*
18	Obcl6		Y		Y	Y		Ermp	ITS/ AffCom	P
19	Obcl8				Y	Y		Ermp	AffCom	P
20	Obcl 5		Y		Y	Y		Ermp	ITS /AffCom	P
21	Obcl 5		Y		Y	Y			ITS	
22	Obcl 6		Y		Y	Y		Education	ITS	
23	Obcl 3		Y		Y	Y		Education	CAT	
24	Obcl 4		Y		Y	Y		Education	AffCom P	
Total	**142**	**2**	**12**		**21**	**24**	**3**			
Mukund Pur(56)	**334**	**22**	**36**		**78**	**30**	**5**			
Grand Total(102)	**570**	**113**	**119**		**74**	**35**	**6**			

Annexure 8 : Study of Digital Scenario (Rural/Urban/Suburban)

A. Family (Gen/SC/ST/OBC) : ....

1. The respondent's name/address : ....

2. Number of members : ....

3. Educational profile and age : ....

   Matric/10+2 Graduate /Undergraduate (Science/Arts/Com) Postgraduate

   M/T - G(Sc/Arts) - U – P–

4. Skills/Training Profile if not employed:

   ....

5. Occupational Profile:

   ....

   IT Non-IT Farming (acres of land/farming/horticulture)

6. Income — Combined-Income (IT/Non-IT/Agriculture)

7. Family over heads
   i) House : palatial/good house/shanty
   ii) Consumer Durables : TV/car / mobike /mobile

B. Infostructure

i) Computing facilities(PC/Software/Mob/Digitcam/services) ....

ii) Communication facilities(Telephony/cable/satellite/wireless) ....
....

iii) Content(entertainment/publishing/information services) ....

C. IT Application/awareness

9. i) Among the educated how many members use computers?..

ii) Among the educated how many play games on Computers?
....

iii) Among the educated how many use email? ....

iv) Has any transaction been done on computer/Internet? ....

10. Future Plans

    Trainings/Education/Employment ....

    Digital Economy Non-digital Economy ....

11. The Digital Economy/IT Opportunities(Bright future/Little Future/No-future)

    ....

12. What should be done to enable IT benefits reach more people, and all regions?

    ....

13. Problems related to telephony, cable, satellite, etc.

    Place/Date

....

Place/Date

Enumerator's Signature/Name

....

Signature of P.C. Bodh
(Director Planning Commission,
33rd APPPA Course, IIPA,
IP Estate New Delhi.)

Bibliography

Kagami, Mitsuhiro, *Digital Divide or Digital Jump: Beyond IT Revolution.*

Tapscott, Don, *The Digital Economy : Promise and Peril in the Age of Networked Intelligence.*

Doyle, Gillian, *Understanding Media Economics.*

Turner, Colin, *The Information Economy : Business Strategy for Digital Age.*

Johansson, B., *The Emerging Digital Economy.*

Comer, Douglas E., "Computer Networks and Internets", by Keniston, Kenneth, Kumar, Deepak, *IT Experience in India.*

Drucker, Peter F., *The New Realities.*

Barry, Brian, *Why Social Justice Matters.*

India Vision 2020; Approach Paper of the 11th Plan.

11th Five Year Plan Document.

Working Group Report of Ministry of Information Technology Working.

Group Report of Telecommunication.

Working Group Report of Information and Broadcasting.

Working Group Report of Human Resource.

Working Group Report of Health and Family Welfare.

Working Group Report Agriculture and its Allied Sectors.

11th Plan Steering Committee Report of Ministry of Information Technology.

11th Plan Steering Committee Report of Telecommunication.

11th Plan Steering Committee Report of Information and Broadcasting.

11th Plan Steering Committee Report of Human Resource.

11th Plan Steering Committee Report of Health and Family Welfare.

11th Plan Steering Committee Report of Agriculture and its Allied Sectors.